I Don't Want to Go to Church!

PRACTICAL WAYS TO DEAL WITH KIDS AND RELIGION
(Whether You're Religious or Not)

SCOTT COOPER

Novitiate Library
Mont La Salle
Napa, California

PAULIST PRESS
New York/Mahwah, NJ

Unless otherwise noted, the scripture quotations outlined herein are from the New Revised Standard Version Bible, copyright © 1989 by the Division of Christian Education of the National Council of Churches of Christ in the U.S.A. Used by permission.

Cover illustration: Jessica Wedvick/Getty Images. Used with permission.
Cover design by Steve Scholl
Book design by Lynn Else

Library of Congress Cataloging-in-Publication Data

Cooper, Scott.
    I don't want to go to church! : practical ways to deal with kids and religion (whether you're religious or not) / Scott Cooper.
        p. cm.
    ISBN 0-8091-4398-4 (alk. paper)
    1. Christian education—Home training. 2. Christian education of children. 3. Moral education. I. Title.
    BV1590.C593 2006
    248.8′45—dc22

                                                            2006029106

Published by Paulist Press
997 Macarthur Boulevard
Mahwah, New Jersey 07430

www.paulistpress.com

Printed and bound in the
United States of America

Contents

Acknowledgments

Thank you to Ray Noll, professor of theology at the University of San Francisco, for his review and encouragement. My appreciation to Judy Hull, spiritual formation director of the First United Methodist Church in Santa Rosa, California, and retired pastor, for her review and helpful input. Special appreciation goes to Paulist Press: to managing editor Paul McMahon and his team, and to publisher Lawrence Boadt for providing the opportunity to publish this book. As usual, special thanks to my wife, Julie, for her significant contribution.

Introduction

Surveys and studies confirm that religious influence is good for children and that (predominantly) they are quite interested in core religious issues during childhood. If anything, the interest that children have in religion has increased over the last few decades according to Gallup Poll data. As parents, we have a wonderful opportunity to provide a religious and moral foundation for our children that they can build upon in their own unique ways. In the end, this may be one of the most important legacies we can leave them.

I wrote a previous book on the topic of providing religious and moral training for children entitled *God at the Kitchen Table*. While the book was written for all parents who are interested in such training, it was particularly geared toward providing ideas to parents who might be less inclined to be involved in organized religion. The emphasis was therefore on what parents could do in their own homes regardless of whether or not they participated in church services or activities on a regular basis.

As I made presentations to parenting groups on the topic, and communicated with clergy and others, it became clear to me that there was need for an additional resource oriented more directly toward churched parents, while still meeting the needs of those who might be more or less religious and more or less orthodox in their faith traditions. Thus, *I Don't Want to Go to Church!* includes some of the basic concepts from my previous book, as they apply to all parents, but also provides ideas regarding the value and possibilities of being part of a faith community. This book is meant to be a resource that church leaders, educators, grandparents, and parents can read and share to help families find their way in providing helpful religious and moral grounding for their children.

For simplicity's sake, I have used the traditional male pronoun for God (he, him) throughout the text. When I use the term "church," I use it in the most inclusive sense possible—as a stand-in for all faith communities.

CHAPTER ONE

Why at Least Some Religion Is Important for Children

The greatest gifts my parents gave to me...were their unconditional love and a set of values. Values that they lived by and didn't just lecture about. Values that included an understanding of the simple difference between right and wrong, a belief in God, the importance of hard work and education.
— Colin Powell
(U.S. statesman and general)

To this day I well remember sitting on my sore little bottom in church, watching the clock on the wall as its hands slowly ticked away. I remember sorting through the fuzz in the pocket of my sport coat to find some little trinket of entertainment, trying to get my siblings to laugh, and regularly pleading to go to the bathroom, all in an effort to make it through another Sunday of church. My restless heart surged with relief whenever the closing hymn turned out to have only one verse, and I sat in gloom whenever I sensed that the speaker was going to be long-winded. Nothing was more liberating than to tear out of church and rip off my coat and tie. I can easily relate to the story of how Joe Torre, manager of the New York Yankees, and his older brother Frank, used to go to early Sunday Mass wearing their spikes so that they could run straight to the baseball field afterward.

Things improved. Religion became an issue of greater intellectual interest to me during adolescence (as sometimes happens to teenagers, according to Jean Piaget and other human-development specialists). Although I still didn't enjoy aspects of church, I respected it as a vehicle for faith and for keeping me out of major trouble. The value wasn't so much in what was said in church, as it was being in a place, with family and others, that culturally reinforced ideas of faith and morality. Church was the key nonfamily place in my social learning experience that reinforced the notion that God and goodness mattered. It also provided a small community of supportive "brothers and sisters" who treated me as one of their own. My church experience may have forever ruined my capacity for sitting through meetings, but it helped to establish a foundation of beliefs and values that I could refer to and build on.

BELIEFS AND VALUES

Religion is important for children because beliefs are important. Beliefs are like mental blueprints that strongly influence our everyday attitudes, thoughts, emotions, and actions. They influence what we really care about—that is, our values—and provide us with our rules for living. Beliefs can be our springboards, by giving us hope, freedom, discipline, and perspective; or our prisons, by fostering despair, lack of purpose, and self-defeating behaviors.

Religious beliefs are particularly important because they help us relate to the bigger scheme of things. They can affect the level of hope and purpose we have, and can shape our attitudes about ourselves, others, and life itself. They have to do with acknowledging and honoring the source of life, determining how we should live, and considering what happens to us after we die: the big questions of "Where did we come from?" "Why are we here?" and "Where are we going?" How our children answer these questions for themselves will influence their outlook on life and will contribute to their blueprint for living.

A healthy religious foundation can help orient children toward core beliefs that are positive and hopeful and that provide the perspective to help them deal with life's ups and downs. These beliefs say:

1. *About self:* that they're a worthwhile creation of God;

2. *About others:* that others are part of the "family of God" and therefore worthy of our help and mercy;

3. *About the universe:* that it's ultimately directed by a higher power (God) that we can turn to and trust through the thick and thin of life;

4. *About right and wrong:* that when we choose the right thing to do (helping others and refraining from harm), it is not only a better way for all of us to live, but our duty as part of the family of God;

5. *About death:* that we return to God when our life here ends.

Modern studies confirm that religious people find more purpose and happiness, are less depressed and anxious, and are better able to cope with such crises as illness, divorce, and bereavement; therefore, the content of children's core beliefs will affect their adult well-being and coping capabilities.

In *What I Know for Sure,* Oprah Winfrey writes of sitting as a child in the "second pew to the right" every Sunday in her Progressive Missionary Baptist Church in Mississippi, writing down everything the minister said. At her school the next day she would recite the sermon on her playground, prompting children who saw her coming to say, "Here comes that preacher." She learned the Golden Rule ("Do unto others as you would have them do unto you"), and she carried those words around in her book satchel. Her religious experience influenced the rest of her very successful life. As she puts it: "I believed I belonged to someone or something bigger than myself, my family, or even Mississippi. I believed I was God's child. Therefore I could do anything."

As much as anybody in my own life, my father exemplified the benefits of a life influenced by faith. He had grown up in very sparse rural circumstances during the Great Depression and had worked hard at a young age to help his family survive economically. He then worked his way through college, having his dreams interrupted by military service during World War II, but finally graduating with a master's degree in science at the age of thirty-three. He was the only member of his family to graduate from college. Yet within just a few years he lost his business and home and was heavily in debt. He spent much of the remainder of his life struggling financially to raise five children. But my father was never bitter, nor did he complain about the bad hand that life had sometimes dealt him. Through it all, he remained committed to and engaged in a life of faith— actively participating and serving in his faith tradition. When I look back, it is clear to me that his faith gave him a larger perspective that allowed him to handle the vicissitudes of his life with patience and grace. As American philosopher and psychologist William James wrote in *The Varieties of Religious Experience:* "At the bottom the whole concern of both morality and religion is with the manner of our acceptance of the universe. Do we accept it only in part and grudgingly, or heartily and altogether?"

MORAL INFLUENCE

Perhaps the most important religious beliefs for our children's practical well-being are those that deal with how best to live their lives. Morality is often an emotionally charged term, but the concept is very simple. Morality says that some behaviors are better than others (love is better than hate, honesty is better than dishonesty, marital fidelity is better than infidelity), and that it's good to choose to live by those better behaviors. People can make good moral choices regardless of whether they believe in God or go to church. But certainly a belief in God can deepen a person's sense of urgency and duty when it comes to making good choices and benefiting the world. And church is one of the few places in the world where our children can go to be formally taught clear rules of morality.

The major religious traditions of our time reinforce the connection between religion and morality, and are champions for moral good. When Jesus was once asked what people needed to do to obtain eternal life, he simply said, "You know the commandments: 'You shall not murder; you shall not commit adultery; you shall not steal; you shall not bear false witness; you shall not defraud; honor your father and mother.'" The prophet Muhammad is quoted as saying, "Do you love your Creator? Love your fellow beings first." In recent years the Dalai Lama has said, "My religion is very simple. My religion is kindness." One of the great contributions that religion can make to our children's personal lives, and to the larger world they will live in, is to teach, model, and reinforce rules of positive morality. Children need to be taught to choose the right—it doesn't always come naturally.

This positive influence is confirmed in empirical studies. In 2002, *Child Trends* published a report that summarizes several years of studies regarding relationships between religious involvement and the well-being of children ("Religion and Spirituality in Childhood and Adolescence," Moore and Bridges). In summarizing the report, the authors make the following observations:

- Most researchers have reported that high levels of religiosity are linked with low levels of delinquency (e.g., theft, vandalism, violence against others).

- The evidence linking religious involvement and decreased teen drug-and-alcohol use is strong and consistent.

- Numerous studies indicate that being involved in religion may help steer teens away from early sexual activity.

- Research findings from early adolescence consistently support a positive association between religiosity and socially beneficial and altruistic attitudes and behavior.

SOCIAL SUPPORT SYSTEM

Beyond faith and morality, religion can also influence children by way of social support (more on this in the next chapter). There is much empirical evidence to support the notion that as children get older, peer influence becomes stronger. Peers don't appear to have a lot of influence when it comes to religious belief, but they do have influence when it comes to behavior. The social support system that comes by way of organized religion can provide adult and peer influences that are positive.

Reggie White, the talented football player, grew up in the projects of Chattanooga, Tennessee. He had been born to young, unmarried parents and didn't have immediate adult-male influence. His life might have gone in any number of directions, but his grandmother would walk from her home every Sunday and take him to the Alton Park Bible Church. Here, Reggie found positive adult and peer influence. He participated in study groups, service, and recreational activities, and his minister would come to his home to check in on Reggie and his brother. As a result of this strong social influence, Reggie not only stayed out of trouble, he excelled in school and athletics (even becoming an ordained minister at the age of seventeen). This influence set his life on a course that would help him, not only to succeed personally, but to do much good for others.

Religious social influence by means of a faith community not only reinforces a child's personal religion (beliefs, moral vows, and prayer habits), but it can provide great social support (friends, counselors, and comforters). It can provide a positive alternative to social groups that may apply negative peer pressure. And if we participate in a traditional "family religion" with our extended-family members, including joining in religious celebrations and rites of passage (confirmations, baptisms, and so forth), this can reinforce our bonds of both faith and family.

CHILDREN'S INTEREST IN RELIGION

It's clear that religious influence can be good for children. But the other reason that religion matters for children is that by and large they are simply interested in it. For many years, the Gallup Poll has conducted surveys among teens in the United States and asked them about their views on religion. Among other things past surveys (between the mid 1990s and the early 2000s) have revealed the following:

- 95% of teens expressed a belief in God (whether a personal God, a universal spirit, or a higher power).

- 84% considered religion to be important in their lives.

- 78% were either "very" or "fairly" confident that they would be more religious than their parents.

- 74% prayed at least occasionally.

- 73% believed it was either "somewhat" or "very" important that parents attend church with their teens.

- 67% expressed a need in their lives for spiritual growth.

- 67% favored prayer in schools.

- 49% attended church weekly (although this number varied slightly from year to year and decreased for high school seniors in non-Gallup surveys).

The University of Pennsylvania's Center for the Study of Youth Policy released a report in 2002 ("Youth and Religion: A Nation of Young Believers") that mirrored some of these numbers almost identically, particularly in the area of religious interest and church attendance. The study concluded that "today's youth exhibit the same religious trends as previous generations if not more."

To not provide at least a certain degree of religious influence is to leave gaps in children's lives that they will ultimately need to fill in one way or another. To not provide adequate moral training is outright irresponsible. Our core responsibilities as parents are to love, protect, and train our children. Part of this responsibility is to see to it that our children receive the religious and moral influence that will enhance their well-being and their propensity to do good in the world.

IMPACT OF PARENTS

Dr. Bernard Spilka, an expert in the field of the psychology of religion at the University of Denver, suggests that parents are often the most powerful influence on children when it comes to religion. In the book *The Psychology of Religion: An Empirical Approach,* Dr. Spilka and his colleagues summarize:

> Of the many socialization influences, parents have typically been found to be the most important. There is copious evidence that parents have considerable impact on the religiosity of their children, both when their offspring are younger and also when they are adolescents and young adults....If you had been born into a devout Muslim

family, today you would probably be bowing to Mecca. If you had been raised as a Pentecostal, you would probably sometimes speak in tongues. If your parents had been confirmed atheists, you would probably not believe in God today. If you had grown up in a particular native culture, you would probably believe in many gods.

Whatever faith traditions we pass on to our children, or lack thereof, there is a good chance that these traditions will become their own in one form or another.

Child psychologists tell us that we parents greatly influence all of our children's beliefs, especially when they're young, by our example, by what we tell them, and by how we treat them. As parents, we have a great opportunity to help our children develop healthy beliefs about right and wrong, themselves, other people, religion, and life. Next to love, this is probably the greatest gift we can give them.

> *In these days of world tensions, when the faith of [people] is being tested as never before, I am personally thankful that my parents taught me at a very early age to have a strong personal belief and reliance in the power of prayer.*
> —Walt Disney
> (Family entertainment pioneer)

CHAPTER TWO

The Value of a Faith Community

Two are better than one, because they have a good reward for their toil. For if they fall, one will lift up the other.

—Ecclesiastes 4:9–10

From time to time my three children have asked the typical, deep, religious question that most kids ask: "Why do I have to go to church?" In my less-lucid moments my response is, "Listen, when I was your age, I went to church every week, sat on a hard bench, wore a coat and tie, never went to the bathroom, endured a building without air conditioning in the summer, walked in the cold to get there in the winter, all without complaint, and blah, blah, blah." In my more-lucid moments, I say, "I know it's not always fun; I wasn't in love with church myself when I was young."

BENEFITS OF A FAITH COMMUNITY

A religious community can be good for children. Church participation is another great opportunity to be together as a family. It can provide a bonding tradition that reinforces family solidarity and helps parents reinforce religious faith and good values. Communal prayers, readings,

11

and hymns can give children a sense of God and the sacred. Church models for children our belief in honoring and respecting God. Churches can also provide the organizational muscle for education, wholesome activities, and community service. They can be a place for our children to meet new friends and future soul mates. Faith communities are frequently the first to provide both emotional and physical help to their members, and often to others in need outside their community. It's also the case that for many if not most of us, it's difficult to have the discipline or resources to provide religious training on our own. Churches help provide the support and discipline needed to provide this training without our having to do it all ourselves.

We need to remember that we don't have to agree with all the details of an organized religion for it to have value in our lives. Every day we associate with companies, schools, political parties, labor unions, communities, and countries even though we may not agree with all the details of those groups. We do so because, on balance, they're of value to us and our families.

Institutions can be of great value. Imagine if each new generation had to do everything from scratch, without the benefit of universities, libraries, governments, businesses, and other institutions. Imagine all the lost knowledge, experience, and cultural tradition. As the Canadian religious leader Mark Morrison-Reed has stated: "The religious community is essential, for alone our vision is too narrow to see all that must be seen. Together, our vision widens and strength is renewed."

Sometimes people cling to the view that because bad things have been done in the name of religion, religion itself isn't good. But this is like saying that science, education, government, and about every other area of human interest and endeavor is bad because people have used those avenues for bad purposes. Religion, science, education, and government have all been influences for great good when people have used them for their intended beneficial purposes.

Organized religions may be inspired, but they are nonetheless fully staffed and participated in by flesh-and-blood human beings who have all the usual human strengths and foibles. And because these religions are organizations, they come with all the strengths and weaknesses that are inherent in organizations: the support and opportunities that come with numbers, but also the potential for some of the innate "politics" and unresponsiveness that can come with large formal organizations. They are not perfect, but they can have much to offer.

Studies have identified four factors whereby religious communities can positively impact the lives of children:

1. *Social support:* by providing an expanded network of caring and nurturing adults and peers

2. *Health promotion:* by advocating the value of avoiding drug-and-alcohol abuse

3. *Pro-social behavior:* by promoting moral tenets and healthy guilt responses to wrongdoing, and by sponsoring church-affiliated groups that are involved in community service activities

4. *Purpose and meaning:* by providing beliefs and traditions that help teenagers find meaning and purpose in life, and allowing them to belong to something that is greater than themselves

It's also the case that church and church people can provide a very powerful redemptive force in people's lives. It's with reason that Anne Lamott dedicates her poignant, funny, and brutally honest book *Traveling Mercies* to "the people of St. Andrew's Presbyterian Church." Coming from a very worldly, nonbelieving cultural background (oversaturated with alcohol and drugs), she found that this caring faith community with its great church music kept attracting her and pulling her toward a life of faith and transformation. As she writes, "No matter how bad I am feeling, how lost or lonely or frightened, when I see the faces of the people at my church, and hear their tawny voices, I can always find my way home." Lamott adds that she makes her son Sam go to church, even when none of his friends do, because "I out-weigh him by nearly seventy-five pounds."

The musician Willie Nelson grew up in the small, Texas country town of Abbot. As he puts it, "School was okay but I liked church better." He sang in the gospel choir every Sunday, and these hymns had a great impact on his life. He remembers walking the streets of Abbot at the age of seven singing "Amazing Grace." In talking about this hymn, he says "That song has rescued me many, many times. It helps me believe that everything is going to be all right. The more I believe that, the better chance I have of getting through the troubles." He tries to capture the feel of that hymn which he learned in church in all of his work—to provide some sort of light at the end of the tunnel.

It's certainly the case that poor parent-to-child relation-ships and overly strong peer-to-peer bonds can reduce the positive influence of church involvement, but the potential benefits of religious participation for children, adolescents, and adults are real.

CHURCH PARTICIPATION

Despite the benefit that church can have, we all respond to church differently. Some of us are comfortable going to church every week, some less often, and others not at all. Some of us enjoy groups and gatherings, while others prefer independence and solitude. Some find a sense of certainty and comfort through traditional doctrines, and others are turned off by historical creeds. So much of how we feel about these issues is based on our unique temperaments and our cultural and family backgrounds. It's only natural that we seek out those approaches and organizations that are most in line with our temperaments and personalities.

And it's no different for our children. Both modern research and our own parental experience confirm that children have natural temperaments when it comes to every aspect of their lives. By nature, some children are more timid, others more aggressive, more passive, more cheerful, more moody, more independent, or more assertive. Likewise, some children are more responsive to religious impulses than others. Some have more believing or skeptical personalities by nature. And it's definitely easier for some children to sit and pay attention than it is for others. We need to understand our children's personalities and work with them, not against them. If we try to make religion and church an all-or-nothing, one-size-fits-all arrangement, we risk the chance that our children will one day choose the *nothing* side of that equation. Too little religion, and children can miss out on the beneficial emotional and behavioral influence of faith; but too much, and children can be turned off altogether.

This doesn't mean we shouldn't *make* them do things that they don't want to do. Effective parental leadership requires that we make kids do things when they need to. As Daniel Goleman, the author of *Emotional Intelligence,* points out, "Temperament is not destiny." Our parental influence can either amplify or mute the natural tendencies that don't serve our children well. Overprotecting a timid child will amplify his or her timidity. Not placing limits on an aggressive child will amplify his or her natural aggression. Not giving religious influence to a child who doesn't appear religiously inclined can leave him or her without exposure to helpful spiritual and moral grounding that can be very important to long-term happiness and character. Making a child go to church is no more of a burden to him or her than making that child go to school; in fact the time requirement for the former is infinitesimal by comparison, as I frequently remind my own children. The point isn't that we shouldn't insist on some religious training for our children, only that we can't leave their personality and temperament out of the equation.

One of my favorite quotes regarding religious participation is when Jesus says, "The sabbath was made for humankind and not humankind for the sabbath." This infers an approach to religious observation that is pragmatic, compassionate, and sensible. I'm sure that Jesus would have also been comfortable saying that church was made for children and not children for church.

My wife's good friend has a son who had great difficulty maintaining attention when he was young. She attended church with him most weeks and it was a definite struggle. But rather than fight with his inherent nature, she worked with it. She would take him for walks around the church, sit with him in his Sunday school classes, let him run around when he had to, and showed a patience with his squirminess that was quite remarkable. I'm sure many adults might ask, why bother? Again, referring to the pragmatism of Jesus, by their "fruits" (meaning the "bottom line") you'll know what works. Today this woman's son is one of the kindest, gentlest young men you would ever want to meet—a tribute to himself, but also to his parent's determination to not take a one-size-fits-all approach. He continues to actively attend church.

By the same token, a family's general participation in church also doesn't have to be all-or-nothing to have value. Full-time, every-week activity can be a very valuable blessing and tradition for those who are engaged in full participation. For other people, some activity can be better than none. In fact, in the Amish tradition families alternate between two Sabbath practices. They spend one Sunday together just as family, then on the next, participate in the "gathering church" (by going to the homes of others). I've always respected this approach because of the clear responsibility it gives to both parents and community for the religious training of young people. Other people in other cultures provide this spiritual and moral teaching-influence primarily in the home—either through informal conversations and good example, or through more formal "home churching" efforts including family reading and prayer. The point is that it is not only possible, but much better, to do something rather than nothing.

If you've had a bad church experience in the past, maybe it's worth exploring a new church experience. One of the great advantages of a pluralistic society is that there are many religious options. Church should be nourishing and supportive. We certainly need to serve and contribute to our communities (whether faith-based or otherwise), but we also need to have a reason for participating. If your church experience of the past or present hasn't worked for you, the answer may be as simple as driving to the church in the next town.

MAKING CHURCH MORE ENJOYABLE FOR CHILDREN

Like my wife's friend, we can find ways to make church more enjoyable for children who don't find church to be particularly joyful. We can hope that young children will act like little adults in church, but they won't. We can battle with them to make them sit still at all times, but they won't. Or, as child specialists recommend, we can make their immediate environment more child-friendly. In the same way that we wouldn't expect three-year-olds to sit still in a college classroom, we can't expect them to sit completely still in an adult church setting. They won't remember all the things they heard in church, but they will remember how they felt being there. Parents can do much to ensure that their children retain reasonably good feelings about being in church. Here are some approaches to consider in making the experience more enjoyable for them:

- Take a bag of fun stuff: books, drawing materials, toys, and a few snacks (some churches provide these in "worship kits").

- Within reason, let them wander a bit along and near the pew.

- Make sure their clothing is loose and comfortable.

- Look at books together or color a bit together with your child on your lap.

- If they act up (crying, talking, running, etc.), take them out and sit with them or walk them around the church.

- If they get in the habit of acting up in order to be taken outside, sit with them in the car, so that they aren't rewarded for their ongoing misbehavior.

- If they have a hard time being in Sunday school, go sit in class with them until they get acclimated.

- While they are little, find excuses to make church involvement short and simple—both they and other adults will be appreciative.

- Don't take them to church if they are sick or otherwise not having a good day.

- Have a tradition of a fun family meal or treat following church, which is something of a reward for having been to church.

PERSONALITY AND BELIEF

Children often adopt the religious tradition of their family. But there are exceptions. Sometimes children go in a different direction. This can be due to their personalities, disinterest or boredom, rebellion, or inability to reconcile their family's religion with their own opinions or beliefs. Studies confirm that sometimes children leave a faith tradition in their young-adult years, only to return later on.

But as with patterns of participation in church, religious belief doesn't have to be an all-or-nothing issue for our children unless we insist on making it that way. We all have unique beliefs when it comes to almost any subject. Our exact image of God, our intensity of belief, our views of specific doctrines and practices can be quite different no matter how orthodox we consider our faith to be. It is with reason that there are liberal, moderate, and conservative denominations with very active adherents within each major religious tradition. Hopefully, the organized religion we participate in can offer an inclusiveness that makes room for our child's uniqueness. But if not, we can still offer our children the "big tent" of our own hearts.

To quote William James in *The Varieties of Religious Experience* once again:

> Ought it, indeed, to be assumed that the lives of all people should show identical religious elements? In other words, is the existence of so many religious types and sects and creeds regrettable? To these questions I answer "No" emphatically. And my reason is that I do not see how it is possible that creatures of such different positions and with such different powers as human individuals are, should have exactly the same functions and duties. No two of us have identical difficulties, nor should we be expected to work out identical solutions.

If you have a child who chooses a different religious direction, as long as it is a path of goodness, be grateful that he or she remains interested in faith. If you have a doubting child, simply accept that point of view for what it is. Martin Luther King, for example, spoke of how in his youth "doubts began to spring forth unrelentingly" and of how at age thirteen he shocked his conservative Christian Sunday school class by denying the bodily resurrection of Jesus. But eventually in college he discovered a faith that was comfortable for him and that he could claim as his own—a faith that would give him strength throughout his adult life. Abraham Lincoln usually declined to go with his parents to church, but was entirely comfortable reading the Bible on his own. As an adult he attended the services of many churches but didn't join any of them. On the other hand, former Secretary of State Madeleine Albright was more religious than her parents. She would regularly walk her sister to church and loved attending Mass. When she played, she would sometimes pretend that she was a priest.

As parents we may want our children to own our beliefs and religious practices, but we can't count on it. They're not, after all, us. We all believe what we can believe, and beliefs can change over time. The important thing is to make sure we know what we believe and to share our perspectives when appropriate. Even more important is to maintain a good, warm relationship with our children no matter where their beliefs may take them. These relationships will make it possible for our children to return to us whenever they need our help and opinion.

Faith and prayer, family and friends, were always available when I needed them.

—Coretta Scott King
(Civil rights activist)

CHAPTER THREE

Sorting Out Our Personal Beliefs

Seek and you will find.
—Jesus (Luke 11:9)

For the better part of forty years world-renowned astronomer Allan Sandage spent much of his time peering out into space. After the death of Edwin Hubble in 1953, Sandage was given the responsibility of picking up Hubble's work at the Mount Wilson Observatory, measuring the expansion and fate of the universe. Up until the age of fifty Sandage had been a nontheist; as he puts it, he had been an "almost practicing atheist as a boy." But through all his observations and reasoning, he was nagged by mysteries that couldn't be answered in the stars. Most fundamentally he was struck by the question, "Why was there something instead of nothing?" He found it highly improbable that such complexity and order could come out of chaos; there had to be an organizing power. He came to seriously doubt that chance could be a rational explanation for such a universe. In his words, "It was my science that drove me to the conclusion that the world is much more complicated than can be explained by science. It is only through the supernatural that I can understand the mystery of existence."

At some point, most of us are prompted to come to terms with religious belief. This may be triggered by an innate need to understand things, by a personal crisis, or by the loss of a loved one. It may also be triggered by questions brought up by our children. Even if, from the cradle on up, our personal beliefs have been identical to those of the organized religion we participate in, many of us come to points in our lives where we have questions and shades of belief and doubt. We need to reconfirm or adjust our answers to the big questions of life.

EXPERIENCE, REASON, AND INSPIRATION

There are three ways to obtain and confirm belief and knowledge in our human world:

1. *Experience:* Our experience and the experience of others (including scientific discoveries) give us tangible, sense-based evidence for belief. Historically, in the world of religion this has included inner personal experiences, revelation, and miracles.

2. *Reason:* Our reasoning ability allows us to use logic, judgment, and common sense in analyzing evidence. The ideas and testimonies of trusted others also contribute to how we reason things through.

3. *Intuition/Inspiration:* Having ideas that come to us unexpectedly, from sources that are difficult to fully identify, has been a valuable resource for artists, poets, scientists, and prophets throughout history

These three avenues to belief and knowledge are limited, but it's miraculous that we have them at all and that we have the ability to be conscious of them. For Albert Einstein, the wonder of the mathematical formulas behind our universe, and the implied "superior reasoning power," provided evidence for his idea of God (the "illimitable superior spirit"). William James maintained that, for him, evidence for God comes not from the exterior world, but "lies primarily in inner personal experiences." For the twentieth-century poet Robinson Jeffers, God's "signature is the beauty of things." For John Polkinghorne, the physicist-turned-Anglican-minister, he found a world filled "with signs of mind, and therefore Mind." And for eighteenth-century philosopher Immanuel Kant, "the starry heavens without and the Moral Law within" supported his religious beliefs.

In my own life, experience, reason, and intuition have all been of value. I have studied enough to be convinced that a higher organizing power is a better explanation for the universe than nothingness and chance; that mind is special, and a likely reflection of a greater Mind; that according to quantum physics the very foundation of our material world is immaterial, seemingly "spiritual" in nature (according to physicists, matter is ultimately composed of immaterial waves of "possibility"). I have personally known people who have had near-death experiences, including a friend whose heart stopped for several minutes and whose lifelong fear of death was completely removed by what he saw and experienced. I have also known people who have transformed their lives because of religious conversion and practice. On occasion, I have experienced for myself the peace and inspiration that sometimes come through prayer, meditation, or the reading of scripture, poetry, and hymns. As with all humans (to one degree or another), I have experienced the gifts of faith, hope, and love. And every so often, when out in the natural world, I have felt a sense of the sacred, a connection to God and the universe, that has reinforced my beliefs on an intuitive/emotional basis. My faith is not perfect, any more than my knowledge of many things is perfect. But I agree with Jesus, that if we seek we will find. We may not find everything we're looking for, but we can find what is sufficient for our needs.

STEPS TO EXPLORATION

There are a number of things we can do to explore or reconfirm our beliefs:

- To help us clarify our thinking, we can take paper and pen and jot down our current religious and moral beliefs and why we hold to them. Why do we have those beliefs and not others? Were we simply given them or have we made them our own? Are we still comfortable with those beliefs? Are there questions or areas of doubt that we need to explore further?

- We can compare our current beliefs with what we've experienced in our own lives, what we've observed in the world, what we've read, and what generally makes good sense to us now.

- We can seriously look at our moral commitments and vows. Are they the right ones? Do we keep them? Do we need to transform our personal life to be happier or healthier and to be a good influence on our children and the world?

- We can read and study further. Besides scripture, there are many good books on the market these days that make a case for a theistic (God-believing) point of view, a few of which I've listed at the end of this chapter.

- We can talk to trusted family members, friends, and clergy and religious (priests, ministers, rabbis, nuns, brothers, deacons, religious educators, and chaplains) to get their opinions on these matters.

- We can visit churches or other religious groups and participate in their services and gatherings (including retreats and workshops).

- We can pray and meditate and observe our own insights and reflections as we consider things of a religious and spiritual nature.

Another way to explore your beliefs is to ask yourself any number of simple questions:

- Do you believe in a higher power?

- What kind of God makes sense to you? What idea or metaphor about God is most helpful? (Some examples are a good parent, the light of the world, a universal spirit, a powerful and intelligent ruler, the infinite source of all things, a "holy mystery.")

- Apart from what you were taught as you were raised, what religious beliefs make sense to you now?

- What do you know about other religious traditions?

- What rules of right and wrong make sense to you?

NATURE OF BELIEF

As we explore our beliefs we need to remember the natural limitations of human belief and knowledge. In the same way that there is knowledge and understanding that the family dog misses out on by virtue of its being a dog, there are most certainly realms of knowledge and understanding that we humans miss out on by virtue of being human.

Albert Einstein used a different analogy:

> The human mind is not capable of grasping the Universe. We are like a little child entering a huge library. The walls are covered to the ceilings with books in many different languages. The child knows that someone must have written these books. It does not know who or how. It does not understand the languages in which they are written. But the child notes a definite plan in the arrangement of the books—a mysterious order which it does not comprehend, but only dimly suspects.

Our brains are limited, and we don't fully know how limited they are. As Immanuel Kant pointed out, human knowledge can never be absolute. There may well be knowledge, reality, and experiences that are beyond our human capacity to perceive or understand. We are constrained by being human.

There are, of course, positive aspects to living in an uncertain, natural world. Much of our motivation to do things in this life is based on not knowing what's going to happen next. Our desire to create, discover, and explore is based on not knowing exactly where our efforts will take us.

Much of our joy is based on experiencing the unexpected. Our efforts to help others are based on the belief that we have a chance to make a difference in relieving pain and suffering. It's hard to imagine as much human freedom and choice in a predetermined, certain world. If all outcomes were known ahead of time, there would be no choices to be made.

And because we live in a world of uncertainty and limited understanding, there is no need to become a perfectionist when it comes to religious beliefs. We can refuse to believe things that we cannot prove, but if we do so, we won't believe in much, since even knowledge is not ultimately certain. As William James suggests in his book *The Will to Believe,* to reject all religious belief that is not certain is comparable to the bachelor who rejects marriage because he can never be certain of whether it will work out or not. It's true that he will eliminate all uncertainty by not marrying, but he also may risk missing out on some of the most wonderful possibilities of his life.

A belief that isn't 100 percent certain may still be very valuable in a person's life, as long as it is believable *enough* and contributes to happiness and goodness. Instead of rejecting religious beliefs that aren't 100 percent certain, which isn't at all realistic anyway, maybe it's worth accepting reasonable religious and moral beliefs until they're conclusively proven false.

PASSING ALONG UNIQUE BELIEFS

As we confirm our beliefs, we may find that we develop unique beliefs that are different from those of our parents, our faith community, or the mainstream larger society. Regardless of our church activity, if those unique beliefs are important to us, it's important that we pass them along to our children because perhaps nobody else will. It can be very valuable for us to give our children the benefit of our own experience and personal philosophy to help them sort out life's issues for themselves.

Certain beliefs are important to me, and because I know my children will come across opposing views on the same subjects, I've made sure to pass my beliefs on to them. For example, I consciously respond to ideas that I think can be misinterpreted as teaching a God who is cruel or partial. When tragedies happen in the world (like 9/11 or the tsunami of 2004), I reinforce my belief that God doesn't cause specific sad or bad things to happen. We live for a time in a natural world where both good and bad things can happen, where we experience both joy and suffering and make choices without God's controlling intervention. When some people are saved from a burning building and others are not, I counter the notion that God chose to save some but not others. I believe that we are all subject to the same laws of nature while we're in this mortal world. I informally pass along this belief along with my belief that faith in God is trust, rather than an expectation that we will get what we want if we just believe hard enough. I subscribe to the thought of singer and actress Dale Evans, who lost three of her children in separate incidents: "Human experience makes it clear that we will never understand God in this life, but we are to revere all that we understand him to be."

As you reconfirm your own beliefs, you may want to pay attention to those that turn out to be the square pegs that don't necessarily fit into the round holes of mainstream belief. If these beliefs are important to you, see to it that you pass them on to your children, because if you don't, your children may learn and accept ideas from school, church, or peers without the benefit of considering the beliefs that you hold most dear.

> *Remember that you are unique. Your beauty is special; no one on the earth looks exactly like you. God knows you for what you are.*
>
> —Rumi
>   (Thirteenth-century Sufi
>   philosopher and poet)

BOOKS IN SUPPORT OF A THEISTIC WORLD VIEW

Herbert, N. *Quantum Reality.* Garden City, NY: Anchor Press, 1988.

Morse, Melvin, MD. *Closer to the Light.* New York: Ivy Books, 1990.

Polkinghorne, John. *Belief in God in an Age of Science.* New Haven, CT: Yale University Press, 1998.

Reagan, Michael, ed. *The Hand of God.* Kansas City, MO: Andrews McMeel Publishing, 1999.

Sabom, Michael, MD. *Light and Death.* Grand Rapids, MI: Zondervan, 1999.

Schafer, Lothar. *In Search of Divine Reality.* Fayetteville, AR: University of Arkansas Press, 1997.

Smith, Huston. *Why Religion Matters.* New York: HarperCollins, 2001.

Spetner, Lee M. *Not by Chance.* Brooklyn, NY: The Judaica Press, 1998.

Swinborne, Richard. *Is There a God?* Oxford: Oxford University Press, 1997.

Templeton, John Marks, ed. *Evidence of Purpose.* New York: Continuum Publishing, 1994.

———. *How Large Is God?* Philadelphia: Templeton Foundation Press, 1997.

CHAPTER FOUR

A Home Life That's Good for Kids Inside Out

Love begins by taking care of the closest ones—the ones at home.

—Mother Teresa
(Humanitarian and founder of
the Missionaries of Charity)

When we signed up to be parents, we signed up for the core parental responsibilities to love, protect, and teach our children. We live in an age when it's critical to be fully engaged in fulfilling these responsibilities. Our larger culture—especially popular entertainment and the Internet—is not always supportive of the spiritual and moral well-being of our children. Because of this, our personal relationships and influence with our children are more important than ever. Sometimes, to my children's groans, I'll remind them of my responsibility: "I know my decision isn't fun, but I've got a responsibility as a parent and I need to fulfill it as best I can." Of course, I've also been known in my less-patient parenting moments to simply say: "Buck up!"

SPIRITUAL WELL-BEING

I define our spiritual lives as simply our inner lives: our awareness, beliefs, feelings, will power, and values. Spirituality is the degree to which we're aware of this inner life and seek to live it out and strengthen it. For people of faith, spirituality includes our connection to God and the universe, and our sense of the sacred. Given this broad definition, helping our children to develop spiritual well-being includes everything that we do to benefit their inner lives: treating them with kindness, teaching them right from wrong, passing on healthy beliefs about themselves and the world, helping them to develop self-discipline and resilience, and providing them with occasional firmness. The measure of our children's spiritual well-being isn't how much they talk about God or religion, but the degree to which they're well-adjusted, resilient, and committed to helping others and refraining from harmful behavior.

This sense of well-being is strengthened by both the emotional and physical environment of our home life. To be truly a sanctuary for our children, a home needs to be filled with fun, warmth, and parental love and compassion. Our children need to find a safe place filled with acceptance and forgiveness—a place where they're received with open arms and hearts.

Over the past hundred years there has been a fair amount of research in the area of child development. Of all the theories, two stand out as among the best supported by actual empirical evidence: attachment theory and social learning theory. Attachment theory says that from the earliest stages of development, children need the benefits of physical and emotional warmth and closeness from at least one key adult caregiver. Social learning theory says that children learn their behaviors, attitudes, and even emotional reactions from the people they see.

ATTACHMENT THEORY

Attachment theory was introduced in the early 1950s by researchers John Bowlby and Mary Ainsworth. It came in part as a result, after World War II, of child psychologists observing the ravaging effect on children of being deprived of their parents. Such children were found to suffer depression, failure to thrive, and in some cases death, even though their basic physical needs were taken care of. Food and clothing are just not enough.

Research showed that babies form attachments to the people in their lives who are emotionally and socially interactive with them—not the ones who simply meet their physical needs. A child forms a strong attachment to the person who talks to, plays with, holds, and laughs with him or her. This warm relationship between child and key caregiver isn't just important, it's essential to survival and healthy development. The attachment provides the child with a secure base from which to reach out to explore, take risks, and develop independence. Children who have positive attachments when they are young are more likely to want both closeness and autonomy in their lives as adults, and thus to have good adult relationships.

As our children become teenagers, it will be harder to influence them if we haven't already built up a close and warm relationship with them. Rules without relationships can lead to rebellion. Developing a warm relationship and treating our children with kindness, fairness, and firmness build the foundation for a home life that is good for our children's inner lives. As adolescent psychiatrist Dr. Mark Banschick has written: "There is no substitute for being loved by parents who are fair and involved." Even if we haven't been close in the past, we can begin today. There are plenty of examples of estranged parents and children who become closer later in life, due to parents deciding that they are willing to change old habits of relating to their children.

SOCIAL LEARNING THEORY

Social learning theory says that children will learn many of their behaviors from the people they observe. This theory was popularized by Albert Bandura, a professor at Stanford University. Social learning theory is focused on the ways that children learn through observation. Children observe their parents, siblings, peers, and their larger society, and make note of the types of behaviors people use, and which get rewarded and which punished. Bandura's research has shown that children will imitate aggressive, altruistic, helping, and stingy models. They're more likely to imitate the behavior of people who are popular and control resources. As parents we can talk all we want about right and wrong, but our children will look primarily to our actual models of behavior, and the models of others, to get a sense of how they should act. If we want our children to avoid alcohol, we need to drink moderately or avoid alcohol altogether ourselves. If we want our children to be kind, we need to be kind to them and others. If we want them to be honest, we need to be honest in both private and public matters. None of this ensures that they'll adopt the same behaviors, but it's much more likely.

Social learning is quite powerful. All of us look around to our larger society to see what is considered acceptable behavior. We adopt fashions and styles based on what we see others using or doing. But there is a dark side to this imitation. Nazism, slavery, terrorism, and other brutal and oppressive social conditions of the past and present have been made possible by cultural conditions that made bad behavior seem normal and acceptable. Today our children are being saturated with messages from movies, music, and the Internet that say casual sexual activity is normal and violence is an acceptable way of street life. Is it any wonder that we continue to have difficulties with young people when it comes to these issues?

If we want to provide our children with a home life that is good for their inner lives, we must begin with a warm relationship and a solid example of our religious and moral beliefs. While we know that children learn much from models, sometimes we act as though we can make up for bad examples through talk. Those in the public eye (government officials, clerics, celebrities, and others) need to consider the effect that their words and actions—and often the discrepancies between the two—have on our nation's children. We can't expect our children to "just say no" if *we're* not willing to say no. Teens need more than lectures and public-service announcements to learn right from wrong. As the American author James Baldwin once wrote, "Children have never been very good at listening to their elders, but they have never failed to imitate them." Our children need the gift of a good parental model.

If we have made serious mistakes in our lives, it's never too late to seek forgiveness and begin anew. A changed life can be the best example of all.

MEDIA INFLUENCES

As vital as our own good example is, children are also influenced by social behavior on display through TV, movies, and music that is put forth as a model of what's "normal." Children are seeing and hearing things that would have been unimaginable a generation ago. The impact of allowing this to happen is real and it's affecting our children right now. As an example, a 2004 RAND Corporation study concludes that teens who watch significant amounts of sexual content on television are twice as likely to begin engaging in sexual activity in the ensuing year as those who watch limited material.

In the same way that our places of work and education have rules when it comes to offensive materials, we can establish and maintain such rules in our own homes. If we want our sons to have a healthy view of sexuality and women, we need to shield them from pornography on the Internet. (As D. H. Lawrence once wrote, "Pornography is the attempt to insult sex, to do dirt on it.") If we don't believe in premarital sex, it doesn't make sense to allow our children to watch TV shows or movies that flaunt this behavior. If we don't want them to get the idea that violence is routine and comical, it doesn't make sense to allow certain over-the-top video games or music CDs into our homes. As the adult leaders of our families we need to set limits on what we allow into our homes.

We can also counter negative influences by providing the positive. We can purposely have paintings, photographs, books, music, magazines, videos, games, and other elements that enrich our children's appreciation for nature and humanity. If we want to emphasize our religious traditions, we can include our faith's scriptures and other writings, as well as pictures, relics, and other visual symbols that reflect those traditions. Some parents, especially in Catholicism and Hinduism, establish small home altars or shrines with special tablecloths, candles, and statuettes and pictures (of deity, holy people, and loved ones) that are strong daily reminders.

We can't keep our children shielded from all outside influences, but we also don't have to passively accept whatever is dished out to them. Our homes can become the one certain place where our children find an oasis of positive and comforting emotional and moral influences.

PEER INFLUENCES

As children age, they are increasingly influenced by their peers. If we have a strong family culture and warm, close relationships, the power of peer influence still remains but is lessened. It's only natural that children mimic their peers. For example, have you ever noticed how a child with parents from New England but who is raised in Texas will end up speaking like a Texan rather than a New Englander? And of course you know that your own children end up adopting the tastes in clothing and music of their peers rather than your own. Peers naturally have influence. They can be a positive influence if they have good values, and negative if they have bad values or none at all. As the first-century philosopher Epictetus wrote: "It is impossible to rub against a person who is covered with soot without getting some of the soot on oneself." It's critical that parents find creative ways to intervene if our children hang out with peers who are a bad influence. This may require keeping them involved in extracurricular activities (sports, music, jobs, volunteer work), doing more family activities together, or just setting limits on how much they hang out with others. In especially bad situations this may require forbidding them to spend any time at all with certain kids, picking them up after school yourself, or even changing schools.

I have a friend who has been a good father but lost track of what his high-school son had been up to. One evening his world came crashing down when he received a phone call from the local police department. To his astonishment his ordinary teen had been arrested for armed robbery involving both guns and drugs. Unknown to my friend, his son had been sucked into a gang culture by means of the attitudes, music, and "macho" behavior of peers. My friend told me that he has now taken the strong point of view that if parents err, they should err on the side of knowing too much about what their teens are doing and assertively intervening and protecting them from bad influences as early as possible. My sister has provided me with a good example of this. As her children went through their teen years, she knew where they were and required that they be home by certain times—and she would follow up tenaciously if her limits weren't met, even showing up in her car if necessary! Her view was that, as a mother, she couldn't afford to care about what either her children or their peers thought of her parenting style.

Teens are in a strange transitional stage. Part adult and part child, they are quite capable of adult-like activities but are still susceptible to making immature choices. It's borne out by research that their brains are still developing, and that physiologically they can't entirely keep themselves from poor judgment. They plead for our trust at the stage of life when they may be least trustworthy. Spiritual and moral mentoring of teens has much to do with protecting them through this vulnerable stage: knowing where they are, what they're doing, who they're with; keeping them away from dangerous elements; and following through on limits. It's also about helping them to not overidentify with peer groups.

One of the best bits of advice that we received from friends years ago regarding teens was to go on lots of trips together as a family. We observed over the years how these friends would take their kids on quick weekend outings during the school year, and take road trips, go camping, and visit relatives during the summer. This seemed to me counterintuitive. Kids don't naturally want to hang out with family, and forcing siblings to be together on trips had always looked like a big trial. Nonetheless, we tried it when our children were young, and have continued, and it turned out to be good advice. Even the tribulations of these trips have a bonding effect. It reduces the amount of hanging-out time and the continuous calls from friends. The younger you start doing things just as a family, the more accustomed to it children are likely to be when they're older.

It's only natural that teens seek independence and want less of our influence, and we do need to begin to let go and support their growing autonomy. But some level of influence, especially when it comes to their protection, remains crucial. It's a cliché, but also completely true, that our children need us to be parents, not just buddies, at this critical stage.

DISCIPLINE AND HAPPINESS

As vital as parental warmth and example are, they're not enough. In the 1960s, Dr. Diane Baumrind of University of California at Berkeley identified three core parenting styles that are still used as the basis for research in the field of child development: *Authoritarian* parents impose their will in strict and arbitrary ways, allowing little autonomy or flexibility for their children; *permissive* parents nurture their children but impose few limits; *authoritative* parents set limits while accepting their children's uniqueness and feelings. Studies show that an authoritative style results in more positive outcomes for children. Children need both warmth and discipline. Warm time spent together teaches connection and empathy. Consistent and fair discipline teaches self-control and responsibility.

It's clear that a measure of self-discipline is required for the happiness of human beings. We can't adequately achieve our dreams, refrain from harmful behavior, help others, or deal with mental and physical difficulties if we haven't developed a degree of self-control and resilience. We do our children no favors by leading them from one fun event (or toy) to another and shielding them from difficulty. They will be unprepared for life and its trials. As our children get used to forgoing their own impulses and comforts to get worthwhile things done, they become stronger internally and more able to handle discomfort and misfortune. This ability is essential to the enhancement of resiliency and good character.

Teddy Roosevelt was particularly close to his father. Roosevelt was quite sickly when he was young, especially with asthma attacks, and his father, Theodore Sr., would frequently walk him through the night to make sure that he would be all right. But his father also taught him to not shy away from life solely because of illness. He prodded his son to become as physically active as he could be through a regimen of exercise and chores. His father also taught him lessons about the discipline of helping others through his own direct example of once-a-week volunteer service on behalf of those in need. Although President Roosevelt had health issues throughout his life, that is not what he's known for because of the gusto that his father helped him to develop. Few grown men have swum naked in the Potomac during winter as Teddy Roosevelt would do on occasion. And few people have been so fully committed throughout their entire adult lives to public service.

Mundane family responsibilities, chores, physical activity, and community service can do much to accustom our children to forgo impulses and comfort when they need to. These things also reinforce the notion that responsibilities come with being part of a group of people. Family chores provide children with the opportunity not only to develop self-discipline but also to learn to help and be of service. Responsibility teaches children how to put aside their own immediate comfort and get routine necessities taken care of. It's also part of the hands-on training we need to provide them in preparation for their work in the adult world (which can also be strongly reinforced by summer jobs or volunteer work as they get older). Jerry Rice, the outstanding football player, is the son of a brick mason. Rice maintains that it was tossing and catching bricks while on a scaffold, working for his father in the hot Mississippi sun that helped give him the discipline (and quick hands) to excel in his athletic career. In addition to the practical benefits to the family (food preparation, shopping, laundry, dishwashing, yard work, and housecleaning), and the development of self-discipline, chores can also be another good reason for parents and children just to do things together.

Establishing and following through with family rules is also important in the development of self-discipline and positive moral behavior. We need to make sure that our list of "don'ts" doesn't get too long and burdensome, but we do indeed need to have the list. Beyond the biggies of violence, sex, and drugs, normal don'ts include—

- No mean physical contact

- No cruel speech or profanity

- No taking other people's things without permission

- No lying or cheating

- No engaging in inappropriate entertainment or wearing inappropriate clothing

Consequences such as the child's needing to make up for an infraction, being separated from other children, being assigned a chore, or being deprived of social activities can all be effective ways of reinforcing core rules. For dealing with very serious behavioral problems when it comes to family rules, good resources include *Back in Control* by Gregory Bodenhamer (New York: Simon & Shuster, 1983) and *Before It's Too Late* by Stanton Samenow (New York: Crown, 1999).

It's especially important to our home environment to have rules and approaches that reduce the amount of family conflict, both in separating siblings from each other, even teens, and by providing a good example of adult problem-solving. It's natural to have a certain degree of conflict in families. We all have our own needs, opinions, frustrations, and temperaments, and it's sometimes important to stand up for ourselves. But a habit of conflict can corrode the happiness and solidarity of family life. How we communicate with our children will affect not only our relationship with them but also the tone and spirit of our homes.

Family means putting your arms around each other and being there.
>   —Barbara Bush
>   (American First Lady)

CHAPTER FIVE

For Less-Religious Parents: Talks, Walks, Books, and Service

You're only here for a short visit. Don't hurry. Don't worry. And be sure to stop and smell the flowers along the way.
　　—Walter Hagen
　　　(Early twentieth-century American golfer)

A good friend of mine, a Harvard-educated business-man, once wistfully told me of one of his parenting regrets. His two children, when in their twenties and thirties, had each come to him independently and asked why he hadn't taught them anything about religion. "Why didn't you ever talk to us about this stuff?" each asked in their own irritated way. He had provided them with great academic training and had provided well for their physical needs, but he had given hardly any thought or effort to passing on to them some anchoring ideas regarding faith, personal ethics, or a philosophy of life.

Similarly actor Martin Sheen once stated in an interview:

I never lost my faith....I felt for a time that I had outgrown the church. Now it is a bone of contention in my soul that I did not share my faith with my kids, as my parents did with me. It was a source of grace when I needed it. I have been greatly nurtured and inspired by my faith.

According to Gallup Poll data, less than 50 percent of all parents and children attend church on a regular basis. This means that at least half of our population is less formally religious in terms of churchgoing. Whether or not we go to church, as parents we retain the responsibility to provide our children with religious and moral training—regardless of how informal it might be. Our modern, scientific world hasn't removed the natural need and interest that young people have in sorting out key religious and ethical issues. Gallup Poll data suggests that 89 percent of all American adults would want a child of theirs to have a religious education, so if we're not doing that through regular church participation, we need to find other opportunities to provide this influence. There is much we can do to contribute to our children's spiritual and moral development.

INFORMAL CONVERSATIONS

While our own solid example of values and behavior is paramount, we can also strongly influence our children by articulating our beliefs and values, and our affection for our children, through our conversations with them. This can be difficult to do if we haven't ever talked to them about these things. But sometimes we need to break through our personality and existing relationships and blurt a few things out the best we can. We need to be our children's primary guide and mentor when it comes to the issues of faith and morality.

In Chinese culture a daily ritual is to have family conversation around the table during and after meals. During China's ancient agrarian past, everyone would come in from the fields to eat together around large tables. As a continuation of this tradition, families today still sit down together to enjoy meals. Leisurely meals with good conversation among family and guests are expected. This provides a wonderful opportunity not only to build bonds but to indirectly teach children. Ancient Chinese religion itself was centered on the family and the remembrance of loved ones and ancestors. Confucianism is focused on proper relationships and responsibilities within the family and society at large.

For your own informal discussion, a few areas that are important to talk about at some point include faith, morality, teen sex, and drugs.

Discussing Faith

Children need to have the benefit of hearing about our own beliefs and values, especially if we're not formally religious. Whether we're a strong believer or less certain about our faith, we may at least be able to say with confidence that life is special and unique; the universe comes from a greater power (whether we believe that power to be supernatural or natural); and choosing right over wrong is a better way to live. In some form, our children need to hear these basic views from their parents.

Life events can provide us with a natural opportunity to talk to our children:

- When religious topics come up in the news—such as movies like *The Passion of the Christ*; political discussions regarding school prayer, abortion, and the Pledge of Allegiance; or the actions of religious bodies and their leaders—we can pass along our own opinions.

- When a tragic event occurs, we can share our beliefs about God and why bad things happen.

- When a loved one dies, we can express our beliefs about what we think happens to us when we die.

- When we're out in nature, or watching the stars at night, we can talk of our reverence and appreciation for creation.

We don't need to be melodramatic or completely out of character, but we also don't need to be so timid about showing a different side of ourselves that we end up not saying anything at all.

Discussing Morality

As discussed earlier, children receive their cues about right and wrong from many different sources. Since there are so many different models and voices, we need to be very clear about our own moral beliefs. While a good personal example is the best model, we also need to clearly state what we think about right and wrong through informal conversation, just to make sure there is no confusion on where we stand.

This can be done in the regular flow of life. When we read about prominent athletes or rock stars who get in trouble with drugs or violence, we might say what a loss it is for people who are so talented to waste their lives in those ways. On the other hand, when we read about athletes who help with charities or speak out against drug use we can point to their good examples (David Robinson and Steve Young come to mind). When business or government leaders are caught in illegal activities, we can reinforce the importance of honesty and of ensuring that money doesn't become the most important thing in people's lives. Sometimes there are examples in our local paper or in schools of people being unusually honest in returning lost money or helping others in need. These provide a great opportunity for discussing issues of baseline morality.

We don't need to be preachy or to overmoralize (expressing an opinion about *everything* in the news), but it's very important for our children to know where we stand when it comes to core issues of right and wrong.

Discussing Teen Sex and Drugs

We live in a time when it's especially important not to mince words about two serious problem areas of teen life: sex and drugs. Our current cultural climate provides, at best, a very mixed message on these topics and our children need clarity to ensure they understand our points of view and rules on these issues.

While the percentage of twelfth-graders in the United States who have had sex decreased from 54 percent to 47 percent between 1991 and 2003, this remains a high number. The United States has by far the highest teen pregnancy rate of any industrialized country. And if unwed teens are not giving birth as a result of these pregnancies, their pregnancies result in abortions—a practice that remains morally repugnant to many people of faith.

According to the 2004 National Survey for the National Campaign to Prevent Teen Pregnancy, 92 percent of high-school teens themselves said it's important that they be given a strong societal message to abstain from teen sex. And according to the 2002 National Longitudinal Survey on Adolescent Health, teenagers are less likely to start having sex if their mothers are close to them and talk about their own disapproval of teen sex. If you want to give children reasons for "saying no to teen sex," you might consider some of the following:

- 80 percent of unwed mothers end up on welfare— they miss out on much of the potential and enjoyment of their young lives.

- Each year over three million teens contract a sexually transmitted disease.

- Sexually active young people can develop sexual habits and attitudes that are harmful to their future adult and family relationships.

Teen drug use is also a very serious problem. According to the 2003 National Youth Risk Behavior Survey, 22 percent of U.S. teens were then-current marijuana users, and 40 percent had tried it at some point. Active teen users of cocaine had increased from 1.7 percent in 1991 to 4.1 percent as of 2003. Besides damaging personal, physical, mental, and emotional well-being, drugs are much more likely to involve teens in anti-social and criminal behavior. The Partnership for a Drug-Free America reports that teens whose parents talk to them regularly about the dangers of drugs are 42 percent less likely to use drugs, yet only one in four teens reports ever having these con-versations. We can't count on public-service announcements to do all of this for us. Besides staying on top of where our teens are, who they're with, and what they're up to, we need to have frank talks with them about the dangers of drugs.

But if we focus only on illicit drugs, we'll lose sight of the drug that has had the most devastating effect on teens and young adults—alcohol. According to the Centers for Disease Control and Prevention, the use of alcohol is fre-quently associated with the major causes of death and injury among this age group (in the form of motor-vehicle crashes, homicides, and suicides). Alcohol consumption is involved in over 40 percent of all traffic-related deaths. According to the Department of Justice, about 40 percent of all crimes (violent and nonviolent) are committed under the influence of alcohol. In addition, two-thirds of cases of domestic violence report that alcohol was involved. As of 2003, 45 percent of U.S. teens were current drinkers of alcoholic beverages and 28 percent had been involved in recent binge-drinking. People who begin drinking before age fifteen are four times more likely to develop alcoholism than those who begin at age twenty-one. The dilemma is that most of the adult population drinks alcoholic beverages and so the societal modeling for drinking is quite strong. Because of this it's particularly important to discuss the dangers of drinking. According to a study published in the December 2004 issue of the *Psychology* of *Addictive Behaviors,* simple mother-and-teen conversations regarding how drinking was bad for teens' health, and could get them in trouble, were helpful in preventing binge-drinking in college freshmen.

If you yourself drink (about 60 percent of all adults do to one degree or another), it's important to not abuse alcohol and to exemplify restraint. In the same way that sex is not appropriate for teens who are still developing their judgment, so too alcohol is not appropriate for teens who are not always capable of using the best of judgment. For good reason, it's illegal in the United States for people under the age of twenty-one to purchase or possess alcoholic beverages.

FIELD TRIPS

Less-religious parents may find that being out in nature also helps children feel a connection to creation. Simply going for a walk can bring refreshment to both body and soul. For theists, nature is the first scripture, the direct work of God. There is probably good reason that some of the earliest religious rites were connected to nature and the out-of-doors;

with lack of the written word, this was truly the place to see and celebrate God's work. As the Christian apostle Paul once wrote: "Ever since the creation of the world his eternal power and divine nature, invisible though they are, have been understood and seen through the things he has made" (Rom 1:20).

It may be the case that no American ever experienced the sacred in nature as completely as the naturalist John Muir. Muir frequently compared the Yosemite Valley and its surrounding mountains to a church or cathedral. His many excursions into the High Sierras were for him an important witness of the grandeur of God. He maintained that adult and child alike need "beauty as well as bread, places to play in and pray in, where nature may heal and give strength to the body and soul."

Anne Frank, a young Jewish girl who kept a diary while hiding—ultimately unsuccessfully—from the Nazis, wrote:

> The best remedy for those who are afraid, lonely or unhappy is to go outside, somewhere where they can be quiet, alone with the heavens, nature and God. Because only then does one feel that all is as it should be and that God wishes to see people happy, amidst the simple beauty of nature.

With indoor entertainment such a big part of the leisure lives of young people today, it may take a little pushing and creativity to get kids into the out-of-doors. Here are a few approaches:

- campouts and hikes
- walks in the neighborhood
- bicycle rides

- picnics
- outdoor games as a family
- bird-watching trips

You can also take your children on "religious" field trips from time to time. In your vacation travels, you can stop along the way to visit historic religious buildings and monuments, such as the missions of California, colonial meetinghouses in New England, and cathedrals, mosques, synagogues, and Holocaust memorials both in the United States and overseas. By stopping to visit these kinds of historic places, you are reinforcing the idea that faith matters. These places can enrich appreciation for people of faith and their dedication to their religious traditions.

Another way to enrich our children's appreciation for the world of faith is to attend community musical concerts during religious holiday seasons, ecumenical gatherings, and services or lectures of religious communities that aren't of our own tradition. The world is benefited when our children experience and become comfortable with the commonalities of seemingly diverse religions, both Christian and non-Christian. As Muhammad Ali has written:

> We all have the same God, we just serve him differently. Rivers, lakes, ponds, streams, oceans, all have different names, but they all contain water. So do religions have different names, and they all contain truth, expressed in different ways, forms, and times. It doesn't matter whether you're a Muslim, a Christian, or a Jew. When you believe in God, you should believe that all people are part of one family. If you love God, you can't love only some of his children.—*The Soul of a Butterfly*

As people of faith we need to support each other and find points of solidarity, rather than focus so much on what separates us, and our children need to be taught this as well. Ronald Reagan tells the story of how his father once went to a hotel where he was told how much he would like it there because the hotel didn't allow Jews. Upon hearing this his father said, "I'm a Catholic. If it's come to the point where you won't take Jews, then some day you won't take me either." Rather than spend the night in the only hotel in town, Reagan's father spent the night in his car during a severe winter blizzard.

READING

In early America, only about 20 percent of the population attended church, and many children received their religious education by reading scripture out loud in the mornings and evenings. Reading with a parent continues to be a great way for children to learn about faith. Reading scripture itself may not always work for all parents and children (most of the world's religious scripture is written for adult readers); however, there are many good scripture storybooks on the market. Regardless of whether reading scripture works or not for us, books about developing good character and developing the spirit can be a blessing in the lives of children. There are many good books that aren't overtly religious, yet they convey important spiritual and moral messages (some of which are listed below). Schools often include such books in their curriculum to teach important character values to our children, but as mentioned before, this cannot be left up to the schools alone.

When children are younger, it's particularly good for their development to read books together with parents. The

National Center for Education Statistics reports that children whose parents read to them become better readers themselves and perform better in school. As they get older, we can pass along books to them that will assist in their spiritual and moral development.

Here are a few examples of the kinds of reading that can have positive spiritual and moral influence:

Individual Books

- *Charlotte's Web* by E. B. White
- *Horton Hatches the Egg, Yertle the Turtle, How the Grinch Stole Christmas, The Sneetches,* and other books by Dr. Seuss
- *Big Green Pocketbook* by Candice Ransom
- *The Lion, the Witch, and the Wardrobe* by C. S. Lewis
- *Old Yeller* by Fred Gipson
- *Anne of Green Gables* by L. M. Montgomery
- *Black Beauty* by Anna Sewell
- *Where the Red Fern Grows* by Wilson Rawls
- *Gentle Ben* by Walt Morey
- *North to Freedom* by Anne Holm
- *To Kill a Mockingbird* by Harper Lee
- *Billy Budd, Sailor* by Herman Melville

Books That List Resources

- *Books That Build Character*, edited by William Kirkpatrick and Gregory and Suzanne M. Wolfe (New York: Simon & Shuster, 1994). This book provides descriptions of more than three hundred classic and popular books dealing with good character and moral issues.

- *Children's Books about Religion*, by Patricia Pearl Dole (Englewood, CO: Libraries Unlimited, 1999). This is a good resource for finding children's books and storybooks relating to religion in general and to specific denominations.

- *The Read-Aloud Handbook*, by Jim Trelease (New York: Penguin Books, 2001). This excellent resource lists more than 1,200 children's books that are particularly good for reading out loud.

We are also fortunate in modern times to have so many current-event magazines that can be used as morality-building reading material. Rick Reilly's columns in *Sports Illustrated* have provided stories of good character examples among athletes. For example, in September 1999 there was a good article about A. C. Green, the talented basketball player who had, contrary to popular culture in the NBA, committed himself to sexual abstinence before marriage. This was a helpful article to pass on to our emerging teenage sons. When we find interesting stories of famous people who demonstrate exemplary character in *Time*, *People*, or *Reader's Digest*, we also cut these out and share them with each other.

Below is a sampling of faith-based magazines that are meant for children.

Magazines

- *Devo'Zine,* is a Christian-based devo(tional) (maga) 'zine for teens, published bi-monthly. Includes meditations, feature articles, and scripture (1-800-925-6847).

- *Guideposts for Kids* is a values-centered magazine for kids, ages seven to twelve. Faith-based with an orientation toward the Christian faith (1-800-932-2145).

- *Guideposts for Teens* is similar to *Guideposts for Kids* but oriented toward teenagers (1-800-932-2145).

- *My Friend* is a Catholic-based magazine for children ages seven to eleven (1-617-541-9805).

- *Pockets* is an ecumenical Christian magazine for children ages six to twelve (1-800-925-6847).

DVDS/VIDEOS

We are fortunate to live in an age where we can watch movies in our own homes, and therefore have some influence over what our children watch. Since children naturally enjoy watching movies, DVDs can be a great, informal way to pass along important values. It's also a great way to spend time together.

As mentioned previously, it's up to us as the leaders of the family to make sure that we don't allow offensive materials in the home. But beyond eliminating the negative, we can also enhance the positive. We can develop a DVD library that includes at least some movies that weave in values that are important to us.

DVDs such as the Anne of Green Gables series, *Sound of Music, Sister Act, Fiddler on the Roof, Pollyanna, Sounder, Life Is Beautiful,* and *Gandhi* can pass along important examples of character and values. In addition to DVD movies, there are also videos of past television hits such as the *Waltons, Cosby Show, Little House on the Prairie,* and the *Andy Griffith Show* that can be positive for children.

In terms of keeping a handle on the content of current movies and making sure that they're appropriate, you can find a number of resources on the Internet; for example, www.screenit.com and www.kidsinmind.com. The website www.commonsensemedia.org is a particularly good site for providing parent-oriented reviews, as well as lists of recommended media, including movies, TV shows, books, video games, and music. There are also a number of technological resources that we can use to clean up movies in terms of language and other content (see www.familysafemedia.com).

COMMUNITY SERVICE

In the musical *Scrooge*, Ebenezer Scrooge tells the doomed ghost of Jacob Marley that he shouldn't be in such torture because "you were always a good man of business." Marley responds by saying, "Mankind should be our business, Ebenezer, but we seldom attend to it."

Certainly a big part of a healthy inner life is to have a willingness to help others. One of the best ways to teach children to be of help to others is to consciously provide them with opportunities to do so. If this is important to us, this needs to be a part of our children's formal training, as important as anything they will learn in school. It's easy to call up a local hospital, rest home, or community center and sign up your child for weekly or monthly volunteer opportunities. Not only is this beneficial for children in terms of being of service to others and developing greater empathy for those in need, it also has the benefit of helping to strengthen their social skills and in building confidence with respect to interacting in the adult world.

Most communities and churches formally organize service initiatives that can help you provide opportunities for your children. Beyond the area of health care, children can volunteer at libraries, museums, animal shelters, zoos, schools, parks, recycling centers, and municipal centers. Children can clean up the community environment (planting trees, picking up litter), and help provide community education (public-service information on crime prevention, public services, etc.). Children can also help people in the community in special need (the elderly and immobilized), and even participate in fund-raising efforts for worthy causes (always with adult supervision, of course). There are also many helpful nonprofit service organizations that can be contacted for ideas and opportunities. Prime examples are the American Red Cross and Habitat for Humanity.

A book that can help in developing community-service ideas is *160 Ways to Help the World: Community Service Projects for Young People,* by Linda Leeb Duper. This book also has a great list of nonprofit organizations that can be contacted for ideas and opportunities.

Charitable donations are also a form of community service. Helping others can be directly modeled in the home. We can enlist our children's opinions on which charities to give to. We can have them make the telephone calls if we contribute to television-based money drives. We can explain to them who we give contributions to and why—so that the example of our giving isn't lost. We can help them set aside money if we want to participate in a tithe or other church-oriented contribution. When we give a few dollars to the Salvation Army bell-ringer, we're showing our children that it's good to help out. Not all such contributions need to be in the form of money. Schools and volunteer organizations often sponsor food drives, where children can take donated food, clothing, or toys to be distributed to people in need. Beyond encouraging children to contribute to these drives, we can actually take them to the stores to purchase contributions, have them help select something from the kitchen cupboard to donate, or ourselves be one of the drivers to deliver the goods.

> *Teaching is the art of sharing.*
> —Abraham Joshua Heschel
> (Twentieth-century
> Jewish scholar and mystic)

CHAPTER SIX

For More-Religious Parents: Prayer, Devotionals, Religious Holidays, and Sabbath

The home should be a...kind of school where life's basic lessons are taught; a kind of church where God is honored; a place where wholesome recreation and simple pleasures are enjoyed.
— Billy Graham
(Protestant religious leader)

Parents who tend to be more religious also tend to be more actively involved in a faith community. As described in the second chapter, a faith community can be a great vehicle for training children in faith and morality. But some church-going parents will want to reinforce their faith traditions in the home, and not all parents who are more religious are active churchgoers. I have known people who are quite religious but have not found a church that they're comfortable with. For these people, elements of "home churching," or the "domestic church," as Pope Paul VI referred to it, are particularly valuable in providing religious and moral training to children.

In our modern Western world, we have become accustomed to a compartmentalized, institutionalized way of life. We get so used to identifying work with companies, education with schools, and religion with churches that sometimes these basic human activities don't become a part of our being. This might explain why even though religious trends have stayed mostly the same over the past forty years, many serious social indicators have gotten worse exponentially (violent crime, crime in general, drug use, and teen pregnancy). Until religion translates into personal spirituality and personal moral commitments, it loses much of its power for good. The real test of religion is in its "fruits." If our attitudes and behavior aren't any different if we have faith or not, then faith doesn't do us much practical good. As Anton Boisen once wrote: "The end of all religion is not states of feeling but the transformation of personality." For religion to become personalized, it should become a part of the flow of life.

Over a year's time I conducted research at the Graduate Theological Union next to the University of California at Berkeley. My objective was to look at the history of religion as it related to family life. What I found was quite striking. In my research, I found that in ancient times the first priests and teachers of religion were fathers and mothers. The original religious leaders of the Hebrew tribes, for example, weren't full-time priests and prophets: they were the heads of clans. The early religions of ancient Africa, Greece, Rome, China, and Mesopotamia were almost completely family-based, and the officiators of those religious traditions were also fathers and mothers. In ancient Greek and Roman homes, the family "flame" was maintained throughout the day and night as a devotion to deity and family. The family would routinely gather around the family hearth for prayers and religious ceremonies.

The earliest Christians did not meet in churches but rather in private homes. The primary worship unit was approximately thirty people, which included the household and a small group of extended family members and friends.

Part of these gatherings was dedicated to having a communal meal together, which cemented not only faith but friendship.

In Judaism most communal traditions are mirrored by domestic counterparts. The traditional Sabbath is celebrated with candle lightings, a special meal, and children's blessings in the home, in addition to communal services in the synagogue. Passover, Hanukkah, and most other festivals are celebrated in both the home and in community, with certain Jewish family meals taking on the character of religious ritual (the family meal table in essence replaced the altar of the temple in Jerusalem following the destruction of the temple in the first century).

Much of the religious activity in India, Asia, and Africa is still home- or family-based. In India, for example, while the countryside remains dotted with unused, ancient temples, the most fundamental form of Hindu worship, called *puja,* takes place in the home. In Hindu homes, a worship area displays the images of favorite deities, and many families observe a morning ritual of prayers, songs, and washings. Congregational worship is rare. Religion is not compartmentalized and institutionalized for the people of India; it's part of the flow of their everyday life.

Since the 1960s, the societal influence of the family in the United States has lessened. However, evidence suggests that religion continues to play an active role in family life. In particular, ethnic groups within the Catholic Church (notably Italian, Irish, and Latin American) maintain strong family religious cultures. Protestant African Americans maintain strong family religious traditions. (In a 1999 Gallup Poll, 86 percent of African Americans, as opposed to 55 percent of Caucasian Americans, said that religion was "very important" in their lives.) Evangelical Christians and Mormons (where fathers actively participate in the lay priesthood of the faith) are also known for fostering strong family religious life, as well as Orthodox Jewish and Islamic households.

What I discovered through my research is that this home-based approach to religion has been the most fundamental and traditional approach to religion throughout much of human history. For more-religious parents, there is much they can do to weave some elements of religion into the general flow of their weekly home lives (see my earlier book *God at the Kitchen Table*). In addition to the options described in the previous chapter, such parents may consider the following additional alternatives.

PRAYER

There may be no better way to model our religious faith than through prayer. By praying with our children we are showing them our faith, rather than simply talking about it. We are giving them an example of a spiritual practice that may be of benefit to them throughout their lives. Gallup Poll data suggest that nine out of ten U.S. adults are involved in a prayer practice on a regular basis. Depending on their personality and needs, children may find prayer a very powerful and supportive tool.

I have known people who pray every day as a family, even if it's as simple as holding hands around the kitchen table as they say grace, and their lives are greatly enriched by this tradition. What we don't realize in our modern world is what a very big aspect family prayer used to be in the lives of the past. Ancient Hebrews would never eat a meal without first giving praise to God. In ancient Rome, families would offer prayers and sing a religious hymn with each meal. In

Colonial America morning and evening prayer were a staple of home life.

According to British Prime Minister Tony Blair, who is a regular churchgoer, he owes much of his religious training to the evening prayers that he prayed with his mother. In London's *Daily Mail,* Blair is quoted as saying, "Dad wasn't religious at all and after my mum died he was firmly anti-religion. Mum took us to church but not as regularly as I go with my kids now. Mum taught us all our prayers and said them with us."

In the book *The Power of Prayer* (edited by Dale Salwak), Methodist bishop Hazen B. Werner has written:

> Praying in the home is more important than teaching about prayer in church school. If there is no praying in the home, a child can conclude that prayer is something that is done only in formal worship on Sunday by a professional religious leader....Even saying grace before meals can be an opportunity for family prayer.

Depending on how we define prayer, it can take many forms. For me prayer is communion with God and the universe. For my grandfather, a rancher, he felt closest to God when he was out riding his horse through the hills and valleys of southern Idaho. Similarly, Jane Goodall lived much of her youth in the out-of-doors and developed "that sense of wonder, of awe, that can lead to spiritual awareness." Anytime we look with reverence and admiration on a star-filled sky, or a glistening sea, we are in some sense connecting with God and the universe. Anytime we find avenues of peace and strength, we are connecting with the comfort that God has to offer us in this life. And anytime we hold good thoughts toward others, wish them blessings, or are prompted to want to help and comfort them, we are in some sense offering a prayer. "The essence of prayer," said Theophan the Recluse, "is lifting the heart towards God."

From my perspective it's very important to teach a view of prayer that is grounded in life itself. While it's reasonable for people of faith to ask for God's blessings, it's not reasonable for children to expect to receive everything they ask for. Even people of faith and prayer go through suffering and tragedy. Children must come to understand that we are in a natural world, with natural laws, where both good and bad happens to everyone. If it were meant for God to help us avoid all the difficulty that comes with such a world, it wouldn't have been created in the first place.

Also in *The Power of Prayer,* Dale Evans Rogers has written:

> In our humanness we fall victim so often to the notion that God should act on our schedule and timetable and in ways that we can readily understand. There is an ever-present danger that we may come to see prayer as a form of heavenly room service. We tend to lose sight of the truth that the purpose of prayer is not to change God or to activate him. Rather the purpose of prayer is to change us.

So a child might ask (especially a teenager) why pray to begin with? The answer is to offer gratitude to God, to seek strength and comfort, to express our concerns and regrets, and, indeed, to ask for God's blessings. Asking for blessings is a way of expressing our care and concern for others. The reality is that we don't absolutely know what all the possibilities for blessings are (there is evidence, for example, for the healing power of prayer). Prayer provides us a means at any time to express our innermost feelings and yearnings to God.

Here are some traditional approaches and tools to consider with respect to children and prayer:

Talking to God

One simple way to pray as a family is simply to have one family member pray out loud on the family's behalf. Family members can bow heads in reverence and one person can simply address God, express gratitude, ask for God's blessings, and end with an "Amen." Over time these prayers may sound very similar from one to the next, but they still provide some good religious influence and grounding in children's lives.

While my wife and I have taught our own children not to expect prayer to God to be heavenly room service, we have also made sure that they feel comfortable saying and praying for anything they please. And they do. When our second son was young, he would routinely thank God for matter, technology, knowledge, trees, and animals. He would frequently and sincerely end his prayer with "Thanks a lot, you've been a really big help."

Prayer Phrases

Prayer doesn't need to be long, or even verbal at all. Some of the most sincere, heartfelt prayers we will ever express are quick prayer phrases in moments of intense grief, gratitude, or regret. "Help me get through this God," "Thank you, God," or "Forgive me, God" can be some of our most important prayers. Anne Lamont says that the two most common prayers are "Help me, help me, help me," and "Thank you, thank you, thank you." As we teach children to pray, remember that simplicity is often best. Children can understand that short prayers can provide them with strength and comfort without having to say anything more elaborate.

Such phases include:

- Thank you, God.

- Please help me, God.

- Please give me strength.

- Forgive me, God.

- Forgive them.

- Bless them.

- Please help them.

- Your will be done.

Saying a few heartfelt phrases like these can be easier for children than trying to remember specific prayers.

Prayer Books and Hymnals

The psalms found in the Hebrew Bible and much of the scripture of Hinduism are made up of religious prayers and songs. The advantage of reading from prayer books or hymnals as a form of prayer is that they contain thoughts that have already been reflected on and nurtured by people who generally have a true gift for providing inspiring thoughts. They are written by religious poets. When we read from these resources, we not only offer up worship to God, we provide ourselves with words of inspiration. Learning brief memorized prayers from these resources can also be helpful to some children. They can provide children with prayer words that are reassuring and comforting to them, and some children will respond well to having more structure in their prayer life. Within the Christian tradition the Our Father or Lord's Prayer are commonly memorized.

Most religious denominations have their own versions of prayer books and hymnals. These resources can be used for family prayers and can also be used for family devotionals. Two of my personal favorites are *Prayers for the Domestic Church* and *Prayers for a Planetary Pilgrim*, both written by Edward Hays (Leavenworth, KS: Forest of Peace Publishing). A *Family Treasury of Prayers* (New York: Simon & Shuster, 1996) is also a fine prayer book. One of my favorite hymnals is *The New Century Hymnal* (Cleveland, OH: The Pilgrim Press, 1995). I have known of families who are musically inclined who have also played and sung religious songs together.

Contemplative Prayer

Perhaps the most spiritual form of prayer, in the sense of being in touch with our interior life, comes from the contemplative traditions. But these are forms of prayer that usually require an adult level of understanding. Such traditions find form in Christianity (the monastic tradition), Buddhism (particularly Zen), Judaism (elements of the Hasidic tradition), Hinduism (Yoga), and Islam (Sufism). At its core, contemplative prayer is "resting in God," as Gregory the Great of the sixth century referred to it. It is a prayer of silence that takes the form of mental and spiritual rest.

For adults, contemplative prayer, or centering prayer, usually involves steps that are very similar to mediation in the Zen tradition: (1) sit with eyes closed and focus on a word (like Peace, Lord, Love, etc.), a prayer phrase, nature, or other focus of attention; (2) pay attention to everyday worries, thoughts, and feelings as they come up and let go of them, returning to the sacred word, prayer phrase, or other item of focus—mentally resting in God and passing on to God all worries and cares. Thomas Keating has written helpful books that describe the philosophy and approach of contemplative prayer in detail. His book, *One Mind, One Heart* (Amity House, 1986) is a particularly good resource. Another helpful resource is *The Breath of Life* by Ron DelBene.

Another form of contemplative prayer is called Lectio Divina, an early Christian monastic approach to reading scripture as one rests in God. It involves reading and listening internally for insight and comfort. The basic process is to: (1) call upon the Spirit of God for inspiration; (2) "listen" for ten minutes or so by reading passages of Holy Scripture, and (3) thank God and take a specific thought from the reading to contemplate. These prayer forms are not usually meant for children. However, children can be taught that simply remembering God or appreciating God's works can be a form of prayer.

FAMILY DEVOTIONALS

Devotionals have been used for centuries within the Christian faith as a way to worship on an individualized or small-group basis. John Wesley, the founder of Methodism, tells of how his mother Susanna would have a devotional each evening with her ten children, composed of saying the "Lord's prayer" and reading from the Bible and other sources. Susanna Wesley's Sunday evening family devotionals became so popular that more than two hundred people would show up to participate (to the embarrassment of the local minister). As mentioned previously, the earliest Christians typically worshipped in their own homes in small groups of no more than thirty people.

The Gallup Poll has suggested that small group gatherings are one of the fastest-growing religious phenomena in the United States. Families are the most fundamental small group in our society. Family devotionals provide the opportunity to touch base *as* family and allow parents the opportunity to teach their own children and to pass on important values. For parents interested in maintaining a stronger faith tradition in the home, a weekly family devotional can provide a satisfying and enjoyable means of doing this.

I use the term *family devotional* broadly to refer to any formal time set apart to pray, read, share thoughts, and talk together about religious and moral themes. Our children spend almost forty hours a week learning the things of the secular world in formal school settings; a devotional time helps ensure that they receive at least a half hour a week of formal religious and moral influence. If our children don't participate in some form of "Sunday school" or a church youth group, this may be their only opportunity to get a religious "education." It's also another great opportunity to ensure that you spend quality communication time as a family.

In my own family we have a brief twenty-to-thirty minute devotional many Sunday evenings when we are home together. This has become one of our most rewarding family traditions. It's a peaceful and satisfying grace note, which brings the end to one week and initiates the next. The structure of these devotionals is very simple. Each week a different person is in charge of conducting the devotional, which simply means that this member leads in asking each person to do his or her part. The devotional then proceeds with the following basic sequence:

1. Family prayer (as led by one of the family members)

2. A reading or thought by each person

3. Informal follow-up comments and discussion regarding the readings or thoughts

4. A family treat (or game for younger children)

We have also used this time to talk about issues that extend beyond religion and have to do with other areas of parenting and teaching. For example, when our children were younger we used devotional time to teach them skills to deal with difficult social situations (like conflict and teasing). On occasion we've used the time to discuss problems at school or at home that we've become aware of. My wife Julie has been very good at clipping out a story or fact from magazines (like *Sports Illustrated* or *Reader's Digest*) or newspapers, which then form the basis for an interesting discussion topic.

But devotionals can be even simpler. I know of a woman who decided to simply take time each week to read the Bible with her children. Her children ended up with a healthy appreciation for religion just from a weekly practice of family Bible reading.

When children are little, parents can simply read books with them, tell them stories, and have a prayer together. When children get older, and are able to provide their own reading or thoughts, it's helpful to have books available that they can use to quickly and easily come up with something.

In addition to some of the reading and prayer books mentioned previously, here are some good books that can be used for family devotionals.

Good Family Devotional Books

A World of Faith, by Peggy Stack and Kathleen Peterson (Signature Books, 2002). A good book (with great illustrations) to introduce younger children to the many varieties of religious traditions in the world.

Celebrating at Home, by Deborah Alberswerth Payden and Laura Loving (United Church Press, 1998). Excellent book of Christian-based prayers and liturgies for families. Especially good for providing good ideas for religious holidays.

Hot Illustrations for Youth Talks, by Wayne Rice (Zondervan Publishing House, 1994; with several other volumes in subsequent years). A series of good stories and illustrations.

The Old Hermit's Almanac: Daily Meditations for the Journey of Life, by Father Edward Hays (Forest of Peace Publishing, 1997). A great volume of meditations in the form of an almanac. Contains an interesting historical fact for each day of the year and then spins the fact into a helpful spiritual or moral theme, with a touch of humor. This is one of our family's favorite resources.

On This Day, by Robert J. Morgan (Thomas Nelson, 1997). This Christian-based resource provides an engaging true story for each day of the week taken from the lives of Christian saints, martyrs, and heroes.

Treasury of Spiritual Wisdom, by Andy Zubko (Blue Dove Press, 1996). A collection of 10,000 quotations spanning many cultural, religious, and wisdom traditions, including many people from the East as well as the West.

Worldwide Worship: Prayers, Songs and Poetry, edited by John Templeton (Templeton Foundation Press, 2000). This is an excellent compilation of religious prayers, songs, and poetry from around the world and from a variety of faith traditions.

The Bible and Its Influence (BLP Publishing, 2005). A critically acclaimed student textbook that provides Bible literacy to children of all religious backgrounds.

RELIGIOUS HOLIDAYS

Since early human history, holy days (holidays) have been set aside to commemorate and honor important religious events. It's estimated that during the latter part of the Roman Empire, holidays and festival days outnumbered working days (though Romans did not have formal weekends). The most important Jewish holy day is the weekly Sabbath, a day meant to remember and honor God.

Since we all enjoy having fun when we have time off, it's only natural that when we take time off for holidays, our emphasis will be on fun. This festivity can be quite enjoyable and provide a family bonding experience, but sometimes the original meaning of the holiday (including national holidays) can be completely lost. The hazard for people interested in religion is that Santa Claus and the Easter Bunny can take prominence over the core historical commemorations of Jesus' birth and death in Christianity, for example. Religious holidays present a great opportunity for having family fun and for reminding our children of the events behind the holidays.

A rich Christmas, Passover, or Easter tradition can enhance the spiritual life of children and parents alike. As mentioned previously, in traditional Judaism, there is a domestic element to almost all the religious holidays that are celebrated in community. For example, the congregation's Sabbath gathering on Saturday is preceded by family candle lighting, blessings, and a meal on Friday night and is followed with a family gathering at the end of the Sabbath. The congregation's remembrance of Passover is likewise preceded by the Seder, a special meal at home on Passover eve.

There are many things we can do to celebrate religious holidays:

- The old staple of attending a service for religious holidays (Christmas, Passover, Easter, Hanukkah, New Year) and having a nice meal afterward, solely as family or with friends, can be a very enjoyable event.

- Putting up decorations and spiritual works of art that remind children of the meaning of religious holidays (and not just the secular meanings) can help to foster religious awareness.

- In the traditional Jewish home, two candles are lit each Friday evening as a reverent way of inviting in the Sabbath. Christians may want to carry out a similar tradition on Sunday mornings.

- During family devotionals, or during family meals that fall near religious holidays, parents can also conduct brief liturgical rituals. For Christians, the book *Celebrating at Home* provides home-based liturgies and other ideas for home celebration of holy days throughout the Christian year (including Kwanzaa).

- Attending special community-wide services (religious, musical, or theatrical) during holiday seasons can also reinforce the spirit of the holiday for children.

The book *Religions of the World: The Illustrated Guide to Origins, Beliefs, Traditions and Festivals,* edited by Elizabeth Breuilly, Joanne O'Brien, and Martin Palmer (Facts on File, 1997) is a good reference to understanding the traditions and festivals of the world's major living religions. Oftentimes, local newspapers will identify upcoming religious celebrations and festivities in your community. The book *The Family Read-Aloud Holiday Treasury,* by Alice Low (Little, Brown, 1991), provides a story or poem for every calendar occasion.

SABBATH

The word *Sabbath* is taken from the Hebrew word *shabbath,* which means "rest." A day of rest, the seventh day of the week, was instituted by the ancient Hebrews in order to remember and honor God through both communal and family worship and rituals. The Sabbath is so important that it is included among the Ten Commandments of the Hebrew Bible: "Remember the Sabbath day and keep it holy." In the book *To Be a Jew,* Rabbi Hayin Halevy Donin has written: "By desisting from all work on the seventh day, we testify that the world is not ours; that, not we, but God is the Lord and creator of the universe....If the Sabbath on the one hand emphasizes our servitude to God, it also stresses our freedom from servitude to human masters."

For religious people, the Sabbath is a weekly memorial to God. The Sabbath was meant to symbolically mirror the final creative act of God found in the book of Genesis: in six "days" God created the Earth, and on the seventh he rested. Rest was viewed as the final creative act of God.

Whether we're more-religious or less-religious, setting aside a day, half-day, or moments of rest can be critical to living a full, balanced, and healthy life. The opposite of too little ease can be *dis-ease*. In our modern Western culture we often find that champions of commerce and industry are praised and rewarded, but not so the champions of balanced living. We are socialized to *have* more and more, but, as the Emperor Marcus Aurelius once wrote, "very little indeed is necessary for living a happy life." Perhaps most essential to a happy life is to have the ability to let go, accept, share, and be content—all related to a relaxation of our attitudes and behavior.

John Muir once wrote:

> Our crude civilization engenders a multitude of wants, and law-givers are ever at their wit's end devising. The hall and the theater…have been invented, and compulsory education. Why not add compulsory recreation? Our forefathers forged chains of duty and habit, which bind us notwithstanding our boasted freedom, and we ourselves in desperation add link to link, groaning and making medicinal laws for relief. Yet few think of pure rest or the healing power of Nature.
>
> —*John of the Mountains*

A Sabbath can be a day, or a portion of day, when we indeed let go of our duties and habits, slow down, and simply enjoy life with our loved ones. It can be a day to worship God, participate in our faith community, enjoy nature, and generally unload our burdens and cares. It's a particularly good time to be with family. In my own case, we have found great benefit to being together mostly just as family on this one day of the week. Not only does it enhance family solidarity, but it provides a peaceful means to recharge at the end of the week before the beginning of a new one.

For our own well-being and the well-being of our children, we need to weave rest and peacefulness into the cycles of our lives. This is important for both our spiritual and physical well-being. It's true that we need to get things done in life. We need to provide for our physical needs and help others. But we can prioritize and we can determine when good enough is indeed enough. We can live with less and make room for family, friends, and rest.

As Wayne Muller writes in his helpful book *Sabbath: Restoring the Sacred Rhythm of Rest*:

> The wisdom of Sabbath time is that at a prescribed moment, it is time to stop. We cannot wait until we are finished, because we are never finished. We cannot wait until we have everything we need, because the mind is seduced by endlessly multiplying desires. We cannot wait until things slow down, because the world is moving faster and faster, and we cannot be left behind. There are always a million good reasons to keep going, and never a good reason to stop.

It's usually easier to rest physically than it is to rest mentally. You can always laze around a couch, but it's not automatic to relax your mind from its tendency to race around. To rest internally we need to learn to practice letting go, if only for moments at a time, of all of our problems and worries. For Buckminster Fuller, who had gone through a major financial failure and was contemplating suicide, this meant pretending as though he had already died. Being "dead" he was then free to go around without any problems and become a "gift to the universe." For many people, being absorbed in something they love to do can help provide this rest. Practitioners of meditation use their meditation practice as a means to help them learn to relax their minds and let go of unnecessarily burdensome thoughts and feelings. If our souls are burdened with real life problems that need to be solved, then we certainly need to develop solutions and move forward. But even in those cases it isn't essential to churn over problems; we need to take action, get help if needed, and not ignore our need for rest. Through all life's events we need to find restful Sabbath moments that will provide the balm to soothe our souls.

> *With religion as a part of daily life, a child gradually develops an understanding of faith...a feeling for what it really is.*
>
> —Dick Van Dyke
> (American actor)

CHAPTER SEVEN

Finding Harmony in an Interfaith Family

A man shall leave his father and mother and be joined to his wife and the two shall become one.
—Jesus (Matt 19:5)

It's only natural when two people come together in marriage that they will have differing beliefs. To one degree or another we all have interfaith and intercultural marriages. Even if we come from the exact same faith tradition, or ethnic or cultural background, we will bring with us the differences of our own personalities, family influences, and individual preferences. Even people within the same religion have unique points of view and feelings about doctrines, practices, and approaches to rules and rituals. However, it's certainly true that there are often greater gaps in unity when the faith traditions aren't in the same "religious family." It's probably easier, for example, for Protestants and Catholics to find common ground than Christians and Muslims. But parents can make the interfaith experience work if they're willing to deal with it—and many have. According to the excellent resource *The Interfaith Family Guidebook* by Joan Hawkshurst, there have not been many studies on interfaith families over the past few decades, but about four of the major ones she says, "All of these studies have found children of interfaith families to be generally well-adjusted and nonsymptomatic. All of the four studies have failed to support the claim that interfaith marriages have a negative impact on children's adjustment."

CLARITY AND HARMONY

Experts in the field of interfaith parenting are very clear on what children need in this situation: *clarity* and *harmony*. Surveys of interfaith children suggest they are quite adaptive to diverse approaches to religion, as long as they know what those approaches are. The worst thing that parents can do for young children is to be divisive on this issue, to let the children decide which way to go, or to not give them any direction or information at all. Ideally, according to the experts, the issue of how to deal with religion and children should be discussed even before marriage if a couple comes from two entirely different religious backgrounds.

Most couples can agree on basic morality. While it's not always easy to sort out family rules about homework, chores, TV allotment, etiquette, and discipline, parents need to be obviously united on the big moral issues of violence, stealing, drugs, honesty, and sex. Finding harmony when it comes to religious belief is not usually as clear-cut. While it is clear that violence will hurt somebody and get the offender in trouble, is there only one way to properly think about God or about religious rituals and duty? Since this is an area of belief rather than behavior, parents of differing beliefs need to sit down and work through exactly how they will handle religious activity and education. According to experts in the field of interfaith family life, it's critical that spouses are honest and forthright about differences. It's much preferred to acknowledge differences, and then to come up with a conscious game plan as to how to harmoniously provide religious influence, than to pretend that the differences aren't there or to fight over them. Spouses need to find common ground and workable solutions for the benefit of their children.

We need to keep in mind a few core principles when it comes to dealing with our children if we have differences in religious belief (or any other issue for that matter). We need to—

- Honor and support each other;

- Determine and emphasize the beliefs we hold in common;

- Explain our differences with respect for our spouse's beliefs (particularly avoiding belittling each other).

APPROACHES FOR INTERFAITH RELIGIOUS ACTIVITY

Here are some additional thoughts, based in part on the ideas of interfaith specialists:

- *It's important to offer our children a primary religious identity as God's children.* This identity binds us to other people (including members of our own family). Our secondary identities as Catholic, Protestant, Jew, or Muslim, or within another formal religious affiliation, are important, but if those identities are too strong they can separate us from others. The purpose of all the world's religions is to point us to God and to honor his creation (including his other children). If we overidentify with our formal faith traditions, we can soon see others outside of our group as strangers, foreigners, and competitors— opposed to fellow members of the family of God.

- *Whether we participate in one tradition, two traditions, or no traditions, and whether we're more religious or less religious, we need to provide some religious and moral training directly in our own homes.* This can be as informal or formal as we want it to be, but first and foremost, our children need to see our own examples and hear our own opinions and beliefs. We cannot leave this "heavy lifting" completely to others. Regardless of how we deal with our traditional faith backgrounds, we need to first determine what we fundamentally want our children to learn. For some interfaith families, formal instruction at home has been a preferred means of dealing with religion. This provides for customized training that can help smooth over contradictions in faith backgrounds.

- *According to experts, many interfaith couples choose to select one of their traditions as the primary "family religion."* This approach definitely reduces confusion and enhances clarity and harmony. It can also make sense if one of the parents has a stronger religious identity than the other. However, it's important in this case for the parent from the primary religion to be supportive of his or her spouse and to be respectful of the other's tradition around their children. For example, my friends bring to their mixed marriage Catholicism and Protestantism. They have cooperatively chosen to make a Protestant church their "family" church. However, because the husband remains close to his Catholic roots, the wife insists that their children have attended Catholic high school. They have emphasized what they hold in common and have provided a unified and respectful approach to religious activity.

- *Other interfaith couples decide to completely unify their interests behind a single "family religion" if their beliefs are close enough.* As another example, a friend of mine was a Protestant and her husband was Catholic. At first she allowed her husband to take the lead with respect to the religious identity and education of their children. But she ultimately chose to formally convert to Catholicism. She was sufficiently comfortable with Catholic beliefs to do this, but she was also strongly motivated to support her husband and children and to provide even greater unity to family life.

- *If one parent is a theist and the other an agnostic or nontheist it's particularly important to sit down and come up with a game plan.* It's critical to not ridicule or talk down to the other's beliefs. Beyond finding common ground on core moral values to be passed on to children, it's also important to gain some understanding on *how much* of a religious nature can be passed on. Religious beliefs can have a real impact on a child's life—in terms of both behavior and outlook. Religion isn't simply a school subject, it's a worldview. For many people, religion provides a wellspring of hope and meaning. Agnostic or nontheistic parents need to consider the potential need for this in their children's lives.

Another friend of mine was raised as a Catholic but made the choice to raise her children in the Jewish faith—the faith of her husband's family—even though he wasn't actively involved in religion himself. She believes in an afterlife and he does not. But he is willing to let her share her beliefs freely. She was faced with their differences in an important way with the death of her father-in-law. She proceeded to share her beliefs with her children in their time of mourning, but did so in a manner that did not belittle her husband. She spoke of her heartfelt belief about continued life after death, but went on to say in essence, "Look, Dad and I have different beliefs on this matter. My beliefs are important to me and give me strength in times like this."

- *There are a growing number of parents who are strong in their respective faiths and choose to raise their children in both traditions.* If there is clarity on what's going on, this can work. In *Between Two Worlds: Choices for Grown Children of Jewish-Christian Parents,* Leslie Goodman-Malamuth and Robin Margolis, who were both raised in interfaith families, comment on what it's like to be raised in a dual-tradition home: "We inevitably reflect both heritages, as surely as we have inherited one parent's perfect teeth and the other's flat feet....There are no guarantees about our future religious or ethnic identities, no matter how [parents] raise us." If a couple can't settle on adopting a single "family" religion, it's still possible to participate harmoniously in the services and traditions of each other with an open heart. Many of us have been enriched by the cultures and traditions of both sides of our families—whether religious or otherwise. What might be lost in being able to fully participate in one tradition, can be made up for by the nurturing of a more general faith that is broader and more tolerant.

Susan Berns, an attorney who has raised her children with both Jewish and Christian traditions, tells the story of how her daughter's friend referred to her daughter as half-Jewish. Her daughter responded by saying, "I'm not half and half, I'm like two circles." Interfaith children report not being confused by this arrangement, as long as the arrangement is clear. In fact, they very much enjoy participating in the festivities of both ("twice the presents" as some have reported). Young Mexican American children are not confused by speaking in both Spanish and English or by participating in the cultures of both Mexico and the United States, and this can also be the case for interfaith families.

• *Finally, sometimes it makes complete sense for a couple to move from their two traditions to a third one of their own choosing.* If their traditions are getting in the way of their love and unity, a third tradition can provide a "family religion" that is the basis for greater harmony. I've known people, for example, who have chosen together to move from their two more-conservative traditions, to a more-moderate tradition that is more accepting of differences and that allows greater freedom for personal belief.

DEALING WITH GRANDPARENTS

Dealing with interfaith issues can be helped or hindered by extended family, in particular grandparents. Once you've sorted out how you will go about raising your interfaith children, it's important to share your approach with parents and in-laws. Extended family can consciously or unconsciously undermine your efforts if your approach isn't made clear to them or if they disagree with it.

It's important for each parent to sit down with his or her own parents, to explain to them the direction you're heading in, and to ask them to respect differences in faith and traditions. My friend who was raised a Catholic, but who chose to raise her children in her husband's Jewish faith, had to deal with the fact that her family didn't accept her choice. Her parents would send her explicitly religious cards and ornaments during the Christmas season, and her sister would ask her if she was going to have her children baptized as Catholics "just in case." My friend patiently but assertively helped her family to ultimately accept her choice, and she educated them regarding the traditions and observances of her adopted faith. Indeed, her father attended his first Passover Seder when he was in his seventies.

Grandparents must be brought to understand that if they want to have good relationships with their grandchildren, they need to have good relationships with their sons- and daughters-in-law. Whether it means formally going out to dinner together to talk, or informally discussing it on the telephone, it's the responsibility of each spouse to make sure that his or her respective parents clearly understand the direction that they've chosen.

> *Do not allow the slightest trace of malice to enter your mind toward any manifestation of God or toward any practitioner who attempts to live in harmony with the Divine Manifestation.*
> —Ramakrishna
> (Nineteenth-century Hindu sage)

CHAPTER EIGHT

Helping Children Deal with Science and Religion in the Twenty-first Century

Science can purify religion from error and superstition; religion can purify science from idolatry and false absolutes.

—Pope John Paul II
(Catholic religious leader)

I consider myself to be a pro-science kind of person. I'm grateful for the scientific revolution and for the many benefits that have come to our human world as a result. I'm innately fascinated by new discoveries in the natural world and theories relating to the cosmos. I enjoy reading scientific journals, and when I'm in doubt about important practical issues (health, public policy, etc.), I find myself drawn to scientific findings and studies to help me sort things out. My belief in God is strongly supported by evidence coming out of the natural sciences. But it's also clear to me that sometimes philosophers, scientists, and others promote nontheistic beliefs, while still acting as though they're talking about science. For the well-being of our children, it's important for them to understand both the benefits and limits of science. Our children need to understand that not everything that scientists say is scientific.

WORLDVIEWS

The problem with science as it relates to our children's religious beliefs isn't science itself, but the worldview that is sometimes passed along by those involved in scientific disciplines. This isn't an issue of science, but an issue of faith.

There are basically two large worldviews: (1) that there is a God (or other greater power) behind the universe; and (2) that the natural world is all there is. The first worldview is the religious or traditional worldview. It teaches that something greater than ourselves has created the universe, that there is an ultimate purpose to this creation, and that spirit is foundational. The second view teaches that the material world is all that there is, and that it has resulted by chance. Sometimes people attempt to talk of the second worldview as though it were something other than a belief, but that is what it is: a belief, sometimes called "naturalism" or "materialism." And sometimes science itself becomes an object of worship and belief rather than simply a method to test theories (this belief system is sometimes called "scientism"). Since neither theism nor nontheism can be absolutely proven physically, both worldviews are ultimately paths of faith. We need to make sure that our children clearly understand that we all walk by faith, scientist and nonscientist alike, no matter how we try to convince ourselves otherwise.

TALKING TO CHILDREN ABOUT SCIENCE AND FAITH

It's only natural that children will be influenced by science as they sort out their beliefs. But it's important that they use sound thinking as they do so. They (and we) need to remember that science is limited to the *testable* and the *repeatable*. They also need to remember that we as humans are limited by our minds, senses, and experience—we simply don't know what kind of knowledge or reality lies beyond human experience.

Some ideas that pass for science, in the strictest sense of the word, are neither testable nor repeatable. Our theory of gravity is a sound scientific theory because we can continue to throw apples into the air: if we see them continue to fall back to the earth, our theory is confirmed. However, how can we possibly prove (or disprove) that the Earth was started by a particular chemical reaction or that there are unseen universes in addition to the one we occupy? We can offer evidence and speculation but we can't carry out a confirming test. Even major theories like the Big Bang and macroevolution fall short of being fully scientific. Science isn't so much a method of reaching truth (which ultimately requires reasoning and judgment), as it is a means of eliminating error. Theories about the past and future are sometimes said to be fully scientific, when they are really best guesses. This is where belief and faith enter in. Belief is a judgment of the available evidence in front of us, and faith is a commitment to that belief.

Fortunately it hasn't come up often, but my children have sometimes brought home ideas from school that seemingly provide "scientific" explanations of life and the universe and leave God out of the picture. I then remind my children of the limits of science (and of how "absolutely certain" each generation's scientific theories and books always are, only to be replaced by the next generation's "really, really, *absolutely* certain" theories and books). I also restate my abiding belief in the creative power of God over the possibility that nothingness and chance have creative power. Sometimes I give my children the benefit of new findings in science (since scientific theories are constantly changing and textbooks are often not up-to-date with new findings). But rather than wade through all the detail, I most often simply reinforce my core worldview: that whatever the processes involved in the natural world (evolution or not), I have a strong belief in the ultimate organizing force of the universe (God). I can't keep up with everything myself, and ultimately it wouldn't affect my core worldview even if I could.

Here are some phrases that I have used in reinforcing faith when I fear that teachers or textbooks are leaving God out of the picture:

- "Scientists make educated guesses about the past, but nobody knows for sure how everything got here; for me it doesn't really matter because for me *something* has to be behind it all, and that something is God."

- "The laws, design, and details of the universe and life are way too complicated and amazing to explain by chance. Many scientists also believe this. For me an organizing power is a much-better explanation than saying that this all happened by accident."

- "Science is great, but it's important not to just automatically believe scientists' explanations. We need to investigate what they tell us and remember that on the big questions of life we all walk by faith—even scientists."

- "Our scientific knowledge about the past and future is limited since many past events can't be

repeated and future events can't be fully
known."

SCIENCE AS A SUPPORT TO THE
RELIGIOUS WORLDVIEW

Any subscriber to *Scientific American* or *New Scientist* is
struck by ongoing changes in the best guesses of science. In
his book *A Brief History of Time,* physicist Stephen Hawking
celebrated the idea of a "theory of everything" that would
unify the forces of nature. He argued that it would be a tri-
umph of science for "then we would know the mind of God."
Fifteen years later he reversed direction and told an audience
at the University of California at Davis that "maybe it's not
possible to formulate the theory of the universe in a finite
number of statements." Maybe, he concluded, it's not possible for humans to comprehend the "mind of God" after all.

As another example of changing ideas, for years one of
the two cornerstones of evolutionary theory has been random mutation (the other being natural selection). This is the
notion that changes in species happen through the random
mutation of the genetic codes of living things. But increasingly the evidence in scientific circles is pointing to muta-
tions that can only go in certain directions (which sounds a
lot like preprogramming already built into the genetic code).
Princeton University and the University of Wisconsin conducted separate convergence studies on insects showing that
nature comes up with similar evolutionary solutions in all
parts of the world, completely independent of each other. In
New Scientist in August 2003, Michael Richardson of
Leiden University in the Netherlands commented on these
convergence studies: "Something about the way in which an

animal is put together limits its options. It supports the whole idea of developmental constraints. In other words, there are only a certain number of pathways that evolution can go down." Cambridge University evolutionary paleontologist Simon Conway Morris believes that convergence is so fundamental to evolution that, given the same mixture of environment and molecules in other places, life would turn out much the same in those places as it has on Earth.

The many not-fully-scientific proofs that are undertaken in the world can be convincing and valuable to pursue, but unless an idea is fully testable and verifiable, it can't be conclusive scientifically and will be subject to possible change. Nonetheless, from my perspective scientific pursuits show an amazing amount of evidence for God. It would take a much greater leap of faith for me to believe that the universe with all its enormity, complexity, synchronization, and mathematical basis randomly happened out of chaos without a First Cause. It is quite easy to believe that there has been a powerful organizing force behind our existence, and, in fact, there is a growing belief that information preceded physical matter: that matter may be, after all, a form of organized information ("It from bit," as physicist John Archibald Wheeler coined it). Quantum physics has replaced classical physics when it comes to matter at the subatomic level, where all the rules change. Quantum physics demonstrates that matter is really made up of immaterial waves (having no mass or energy) that only become physical particles when they are observed. Unlike light waves, which contain energy, quantum waves (the basis for all matter) contain nothing except immaterial information. "The universe begins to look more like a great thought, than a great machine," wrote Sir James Jeans, the British physicist and mathematician. As he further stated, "The universe shows evidence of a designing or controlling power that has something in common with our own individual minds." It is quite miraculous that here we sit as living beings able to participate in the world of mind and ideas. For theists, our own ability to design and create tells us that a supreme Mind could create supremely. Our own innate sense of there being a right and a wrong points to a higher moral law.

The universe has a built-in bias for life and consciousness, and scientists have increasingly made note of the precise fine-tuning of this bias:

- Without physical laws to begin with, there would be no organized existence—all would be chaos.

- If there were more than three dimensions with respect to space, planets wouldn't stay in orbit; if fewer than three dimensions, humans wouldn't have organs.

- If gravity were slightly weaker, planets would not have formed; if stronger, they would have been too hot for life to form.

- If atomic forces had been slightly stronger or weaker, there would be no chemistry to sustain life.

As physicist Paul Davies has written: "The really amazing thing is not that life on Earth is balanced on a knife-edge, but that the entire universe is balanced on a knife-edge, and would be total chaos if any of the natural constants were off even slightly." The complete list of the physical constants that needed to be in place in precise ways for the universe to come into existence and to create and sustain life is quite long. Michael Turner, an astrophysicist from the University of Chicago, describes the precision of this fine-tuning with this example: "The precision is as if one could throw a dart across the entire universe and hit a bull's-eye one millimeter in diameter on the other side."

Similarly, British astronomer and mathematician Sir Fred Hoyle has stated that the notion of the universe happening by chance is about as likely as a Boeing 747 aircraft being completely assembled as a result of a tornado striking a junkyard. To quote him further:

> A commonsense interpretation of the facts suggests that a superintellect has monkeyed with physics, as well as chemistry and biology, and that there are no blind forces worth speaking about in nature. The numbers that one calculates from the facts seem to me so overwhelming as to put the conclusion beyond question.

With respect to life, Ilya Prigogine, a recipient of two Nobel prizes in chemistry, puts it even more starkly: "The statistical probability that organic structures and the most precisely harmonized reactions that typify living organisms would be generated by accident, is zero."

It's difficult to observe the precision of life, understand that it's virtually impossible statistically that the universe could have happened by coincidence, and not conclude that intention is behind it all. Some scientists, trying to get around this common-sense conclusion, have proposed that our universe must just be one of many. This may be true (even though we can't observe any of the others), but it does nothing to explain the uniqueness of our own universe. As philosopher Alvin Plantinga points out, it's like a poker player who keeps dealing himself all the aces and then explains it as the luck of the draw. Understandably, his poker partners won't buy this unreasonable explanation. In the same way, simply speculating that there are many universes doesn't explain the unlikelihood of our own. It doesn't explain why "all of the aces kept being dealt" to bring our universe into existence and to produce life.

I realize that the details of the universe only provide scientific "evidence" for God and not scientific "proof," since there is no verifiable test that can conclusively prove or disprove God's existence. But far from science being an impediment to faith, science can be a strong support. British philosophy professor Anthony Flew, one of the world's leading champions of atheism for more than half a century, announced his switch to theism in 2004, based almost entirely on evidence relating to the fine-tuning of life. According to him, biologists' investigation of DNA "has shown, by the almost unbelievable complexity of the arrangements needed to produce [life], that intelligence must have been involved." For Flew, over fifty years of DNA research have provided "materials for a new and enormously powerful argument to design." While he remains a believer in aspects of Darwinian evolution, he is now convinced that a random and highly fumbling process like evolution can't provide a realistic explanation for the development of the highly sophisticated complexities of human DNA. As he puts it, "It has become inordinately difficult to even begin to think about constructing a naturalistic theory of evolution of that first reproducing organism."

The opposite of theistic faith isn't science, but rather nontheistic faith.

SCHOOL AND FAITH

Sometimes I feel that scientists and educators treat modern families as some of the early, overly zealous missionaries treated native peoples: in trying to convert the native peoples, the missionaries showed too-little regard for native cultures and worldviews. In the same ways that missionaries wanted to separate members of a family and put the children in missionary schools to make sure that they were indoctrinated in the "truth," sometimes state boards of education and textbook writers create textbooks that show little regard for the theistic worldview of most of our population. The current conflict in school districts regarding the issue of evolution may have less to do with science, and much more to do with being respectful of worldviews. Whether done consciously or not, one worldview (naturalism) is being taught in schools, and the traditional worldview of most people (theism) is frequently dealt with in silence. There will continue to be angst among parents of theistic faith until educators and textbooks make at least a respectful acknowledgment of the predominant worldview of our population.

In his helpful book *Why Religion Matters,* Huston Smith suggests that at a minimum, before teachers begin discussing evolution in biology classes, they should be required to pass out handouts that say something like the following:

> This is a course in science, and as your instructor it is my responsibility to teach you what science has empirically discovered about the mechanisms by which life emerged and developed on this planet. Scientists are convinced that we know an important part of that story, and I will do my best to inform you of it.

However, there is so much that we still do not know that plenty of room remains for you to fill in the gaps with your own philosophic or religious convictions.

Smith requested that the National Association of Biology Teachers consider this approach but they did not respond to him. In the absence of educators dealing with this in a respectful manner, we as parents need to take responsibility for ensuring that our worldview and the importance of it are expressed to our children. If this is an area of particular concern, we can also go in and speak to principals and teachers. This is too difficult an issue to be left up to our children.

THE VALUE AND IMPORTANCE OF THE "IMMATERIAL" WORLD

Scientists can tell us much about the physical, material world, but the fact is that in our human world, most of our greatest treasures are not physical at all. All great human endeavors and accomplishments have started from the inner lives of people—from the world of belief, thought, emotion, and will—the world of spirit. All great acts of compassion, kindness, and renewal come from the world within. How can one do a scientific test to measure beauty, love, and wisdom? How can one quantify the sense of awe and amazement that one feels in looking up at a star-filled sky or out at the boundless sea? Through the difficult times of life, material objects lose their luster compared to the gems of friendship, hope, courage, and prayer.

The most significant influences in our lives have nothing to do with scientific tests. And while there is no scientific test that can completely "prove" our faith, there are affirmations, from the worlds of both science and spirit, that provide us with much tangible support for our beliefs. Our real-life experiences, reasoning, and intuitive insights provide us with the evidence needed to support faith.

- We can see design in the universe for ourselves, everywhere we look.

- We can look out and reason for ourselves that the enormity, complexity, and synchronization of the universe and life don't come from "nothingness" or "chance." And many scientists agree. Life itself is the most direct witness that God is master of life—both temporal and eternal.

- From the world of science we can consider the numerical (mind-like) basis upon which the universe is devised and realize that the basis of the material world is ultimately immaterial, or spiritual (a view that is supported by our modern understanding of quantum physics).

- We can directly experience the everyday miracles of the physical world for ourselves, as well as the world of our inner life. As Samuel Butler once wrote: "All the works of nature are miracles, and nothing makes them appear otherwise but our familiarity with them."

- We can observe for ourselves the innate tendency of human consciousness to make judgments about right and wrong, pointing to a higher moral law.

- We can experience the power of faith, hope, love, wisdom, beauty, and courage for ourselves.

- We can experience the peace, comfort, and strength that come through praying, reading, and other spiritual practices for ourselves.

- We can see how others (perhaps even ourselves) have very tangible experiences of the spirit that seem unconstrained by the physical world, seeming miracles outside the realm of coincidence.

- And ultimately we can decide for ourselves which worldviews leave us with greater happiness and resilience—a world in which there is only matter and no ultimate intention, or a world of both spirit and matter and God's full purpose.

Since I cannot believe that this was the result of chance, I have to admit to anti-chance. And so I must believe in a guiding power in the universe—in other words, I must believe in God.
> —Jane Goodall
> (British primatologist)

CHAPTER NINE

Handling Children's Religious Questions

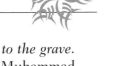

Seek knowledge from the cradle to the grave.
—Muhammad
(Prophet of Islam)

One day my wife and then eight-year-old son Jackson were driving along. Jackson was looking out the car window deep in thought. Finally he turned to my wife and said, "I've got two really big questions. First of all, where did Payless Drug Store get its name, and second, where did God come from?" Needless to say, it was quite a bit easier to answer the first question than the second.

Our children can inspire informal conversations about religion and morality through their questions: "Do dogs go to heaven?" "What happens when we die?" "Where is heaven?" "How do we know there's a God?" "Why don't they go to our church?" "Why do we have to go to church?" "How come God lets bad things happen?" These types of questions can lead to very important discussions.

In order to make it possible for children to ask these kinds of questions, it's critical that we create an environment that doesn't punish or belittle questions. It's important that we demonstrate an openness to listening to other people's opinions. It's also important to sort out our own beliefs so that we'll be able to respond to our children's questions. Our

Novitiate Library·

answers will vary according to who we are and how we think. But while I'm no expert in answering children's religious questions, as a parent, I do think that there are a few basic principles that apply to most of our responses:

1. First and foremost develop the kind of rapport that will make it possible for your children to feel comfortable asking questions. Remember, from the section on attachment theory, that children feel closer to those adults who spend time with them, talk to them, and show interest in their interests.

2. Don't be afraid to simply say, "This is what I believe...," without need to provide convincing evidence. Our beliefs are based on experience, reason, and intuition. A valid intuitive answer is simply, "I don't know everything, but this is what I believe..."

3. If we're given a question that we haven't really thought about before, there's nothing wrong with saying, "I don't know, but this is my best guess..." or "Let me think a little bit about that question and get back to you," or "While I'm thinking on that one, why don't you tell me what you think about it?"

Here are some examples of the types of thorny questions that we're sometimes forced to deal with as parents. I've taken the liberty to identify some possible ways to respond to them. Obviously the "right" answers will vary with each parent depending on his or her heartfelt beliefs. As a practice exercise, consider how you might respond to them:

I don't want to go to church! Why do we have to go?

I didn't always want to go to church when I was a kid, so I know how you feel. But in the same way you have to go to school to get an academic education, we want you to go to church to get religious training. We also believe that going to church is one way to show honor and respect for God and we've chosen to do this as a family.

What happens when we die?

My belief is that we return to God when we die. I believe that our physical body is left behind, and our inner life, our spirit, goes to God.

(If so inclined, you can add something about near-death experiences, for example: "Many people who have come very close to death have reported that they felt themselves returning to God and family members who had died before.")

Do dogs go to heaven?

It's possible. Since God has shown us that he can create life, it must also be in his power to make life continue—even for pets.

Where is heaven?

We don't know where heaven is exactly, but our faith is that when people die, they will return to God, and heaven is the word for where God is.

How do we know there's a God?

God is the name that we use for the Creator of the universe. We know that something has to be the source of the universe and life, and we know that something had to make it so we have the ability to think, to play, and to learn. There has always been something, because if at any time there had been nothing, there would still be nothing. For most people, that something is God, and God has made all things possible. It's just too hard to believe that something as amazing as the universe and everything in it would happen by chance or come from nothing. Sometimes when people pray or watch the stars at night, they feel a closeness inside toward God, and this also adds to their belief. Some people believe that they sense God's spirit and love through their feelings, and some people even claim that unexplained events, or miracles, have happened to them, which they believe come from God. Some find evidence of God through the events and teachings found in the Bible and other sacred writings. Other people who have come very close to death have expressed their belief that they have experienced God's presence. This has added to their belief in God.

Why does God let bad things happen?

We live in a natural world with natural laws. This kind of world gives us the freedom to make choices. If God controlled everything, there would be nothing for us to do, and we wouldn't be able to make any of our own choices. We'd be like robots. In a natural world where we're given much physical freedom, we can have joy and fun, but we can also have pain and sadness. We're all subject to the laws of nature while in this world. And because people are free to make choices, they can do bad things to each other. For our long-term benefit, God has created this natural world, and we need to use our freedom to help make the world a better place. When bad things happen, we can use our power to choose to help each other and seek God's strength through prayer.

I don't believe in God.

We all live by faith, no matter what we believe. We're all limited in this life by our human knowledge and experience. We don't know what kind of knowledge is beyond our human experience, so we all need to sort things out the best we can.

For me, my belief in God makes sense to me and gives me strength and peace. But you need to figure out your own beliefs for yourself. I value my faith in God very highly, so if you ever have questions about why I believe the way I do, just ask me.

I don't want to pray. ᐧ

Different things are helpful to different people. I pray sometimes to give thanks and sometimes to ask for help and strength. Prayer is something that has been good for me. If you ever decide to pray, it's always there for you to try.

I've tried prayer, but I haven't gotten what I ask for. It doesn't work.

Prayer is remembering God and expressing ourselves to him. It gives us a chance to express our fears, our needs, and our gratitude. It's also a time to ask for help and for God's blessings. But God isn't like a genie. So even if we ask for something, it doesn't mean we'll get it. Faith in God means putting trust in God no matter what happens to us in life.

Did Noah really have all those animals on his boat? Did God really part the Red Sea?

Some people believe that everything that's in the Bible is true, and some don't. The writers of the Bible were people of faith who did their best writing about God. There are many good teachings and stories in the Bible. But ancient people also didn't know many of the things we know today. For example, they often believed that natural events like lightning, floods, and disease were used by God to punish people. Something extraordinary might have happened with Noah and the Red Sea, but I also believe that things like lightning, floods, and disease are just natural events and are not God's way of punishing people.

You're Christian and Mom's Jewish. Who's right?

For us a good religion is one that helps people to have faith and to live a good life. Mom and I come from different family and religious backgrounds. We're both proud of our traditions and we think they're both good. They are two different ways of worshipping God.

Why doesn't everybody else go to our church?

There are many different religions and churches in the world. People go to different churches based on how they were raised and what their culture is. If we only had one church, it probably wouldn't meet the needs of all people.

> *The important thing is not to stop questioning. Curiosity has its own reason for existing.*
> —Albert Einstein
> (Twentieth-century physicist)

Some Closing Thoughts

To sum up, here are a few of the central ideas of this book:

1. Parents consciously need to take charge of providing some form of religious and moral training to their children, whether they themselves participate in a faith community or not.

2. This training can take many forms, both formal and informal, that reflect our personal values and personalities.

3. Something is always better than nothing when it comes to religious and moral influence—this is not an all-or-nothing proposition.

In popular culture it's somewhat common to hear celebrities say, "I'm interested in spirituality, but not religion." It's probably the case that when people say this, they are actually saying that they're not interested in formal, institutionalized religion or specific religious doctrines. And clearly, for some people, past experiences with formal religion have not been altogether positive. But it's difficult to be interested in spirituality (the status of one's inner life) without also having interest in personal religious and moral beliefs and commitments. Our religious beliefs are at the heart of our core worldview, and our core worldview can profoundly affect our inner life. Sometimes the term *religion,* like the term *morality,* takes on an emotionally charged meaning that is unnecessary. Our children need to understand that at its core, religion is about honoring and trusting the source of our existence, and living in ways that both bring us happiness and benefit the world. And for many, a formal faith community can be a positive social force in helping us to weave these fundamental aspects of healthy spirituality into our personal lives.

Our children are greatly influenced by our own beliefs, values, and examples. My hope is that this book might prompt a few of your own ideas and actions in helping your children to receive the full measure of your good influence in matters of religion and their inner lives (which ultimately affects their "outer lives"). And above all, it's important that we develop warm relationships and rapport with our children that will grant us the ability to be of influence.